# THE TRUE STORY OF

# Little Women

Most people know that Louisa May Alcott based the characters in *Little Women* on her own parents, her sisters, and herself.

But how much of the book is actual fact? Did Beth really die? Was there really a Laurie or an Aunt March? What really happened to Jo (Louisa)?

In this book, Cornelia Meigs tells us the full story of the Alcott (March) family. She tells us about:

— Bronson Alcott, the impractical and idealistic father, who once brought back all the money he had made on a long lecture tour — $1.

— Abba May Allcott, the mother, who held the family together.

— Louisa (Jo), whose first job brought her $4 for seven weeks of work, and who provided the family with its first steady income.

— Anna, who was "Meg," Elizabeth, who was "Beth," and May, who was "Amy."

An unbelievable story of a brave, loving family, even more wonderful than *Little Women*.

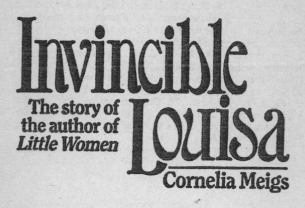

# Invincible Louisa

The story of
the author of
*Little Women*

## Louisa

Cornelia Meigs

SCHOLASTIC INC.
New York Toronto London Auckland Sydney

## ACKNOWLEDGMENTS

For material in this biography, thanks are due, personally, for verbal information from Mrs. F. Alcott Pratt, of Concord, Massachusetts, daughter-in-law of Anna Alcott Pratt; from Miss Clara Endicott Sears of Boston; Miss Sarah Niles of Arlington, Massachusetts; Mr. Warren F. Gregory of Boston; and Mr. Casper Wistar Haines of Germantown, Pa. Acknowledgment is also offered for facts taken from the following accounts: "Louisa M. Alcott, Her Life Letters and Journals," edited by Ednah D. Cheney; "The Alcotts As I Knew Them," by Clara Gowing; "Recollections of Louisa M. Alcott," by Maria S. Porter; "Bronson Alcott's Fruitlands," by Clara Endicott Sears; "A. Bronson Alcott: His Life and Philosophy," by F. B. Sanborn and William T. Harris; "Honor to Louisa Alcott By One Who Knew Her," by Julian Hawthorne of the *New York Times*.

ISBN 0-590-40638-8

12 11 10 9 8 7 6 5 4 3 2          7 8 9/8 0 1 2/9

# Invincible Louisa

# Contents

You can visit the Alcott home in Concord today —
and see Louisa's writings, and May's drawings
stenciled on the walls.

# CHAPTER ONE

❧❧ ❧❧ ❧❧

# Damask Roses

THE HIGHROAD WHICH STRETCHES FROM within the State of Pennsylvania down to the Delaware River becomes, as it nears Philadelphia, the main street of Germantown. It was a well-traveled road long before the Revolution. But even as late as the year 1832, it was still unimproved and often so deep in mud, that, so the residents of Germantown said, it was necessary to saddle a horse to get from one side of it to the other.

Not all of its roughness and its wet, however, could interfere with the joyful stride of a triumphant young father who tramped the difficult mile, on a cold November day, from his house to the big dwelling at Wyck, home of his dearest friends. Nothing could stay Bronson Alcott as he hurried, breathless, to the Haines house, as he burst in at the door to tell the great news. He had a new daughter, a lusty, lively, altogether remarkable daughter, and he had come to take all the Haines children over to see the new baby.

Back they all went with him, trooping along the highway, buzzing with talk and questions, all seven of the small Haineses. They stood, presently, in an awed, respectful circle, around the small, red, but extremely sound and vigorous baby, who, so it was settled even then, was to be called Louisa May Alcott.

It was, therefore, not upon New England, but upon the snow-wrapped Pennsylvania countryside, that Louisa looked out at her first vision of the world. Low, rounded hills, groups of white-powdered pine trees, winding valleys where a black line showed how the water ran, and where smooth, glittering slopes stretched up to patches of woodland — all these were before her eyes and her brisk, young mother's, as they sat at the tall window and looked abroad upon the whiteness of Louisa's first winter. It was not the deep-drifted, biting, Massachusetts winter which Louisa was to know so well later, but a gentle, soft coldness, with the grass always green in the sheltered places, and with the snow slopes broken by upthrusting laurel bushes and clumps of honeysuckle, which never lost their summer leaves.

At a certain hour a door would open somewhere and the two at the window would hear a burst of children's voices and laughter. School was over for the day — Bronson Alcott's school

— and the small pupils were going home. They would troop past down the walk: plump, little German girls with fat, flaxen braids, little Quaker boys in roundabout jackets, who leaped and frolicked and threw snowballs as they all went chattering out of sight. Enlivened by the sight of all this energy, Louisa would jump and wriggle and plunge in her mother's arms, anxious to get down, and very different from her quiet, older sister Anna, who was playing so decorously on the hearth rug.

Abba Alcott, her mother, would take one last look at the broad garden, at the long, cedar fence heaped and decorated with white, beautiful as only snow and cedar can be. Then she would turn to light the lamp; for Bronson would be coming in now that school was ended for the day. Abba had written home to New England that the place where they were living was a "Little Paradise." It looked more like Paradise than ever that winter, since there had begun to arise the unhappy possibility that they must leave it soon.

For two years they had lived in the pleasant, square, farmhouse-like dwelling where Bronson Alcott carried on his teaching. It was a time of great happiness, peace, and security, those first two years of the Alcotts' married life. Happiness was to continue, sometimes interrupted in strange ways; but peace and security were not to come again for a very long time. When they were achieved, they were to be won for them by Louisa, by Louisa battling against overwhelming odds for half her life, bound never to be conquered, even though every circumstance seemed to be against them all. No one could have any knowledge of that now, least of all Louisa herself, the enterprising, small person, rolling and tumbling at this moment with Anna before the fire, both of them turning about to cry out in high baby delight as the door of the room opened and their father came in.

It had been a great adventure for Abba May, after a quiet, staid girlhood, to marry rather on a sudden this tall Bronson Alcott, with his visionary blue eyes, his blond hair, and his finely chiseled, thin, handsome countenance. Certain people had looked dubious and had hinted that the young man was "not very practical," and that he would never "make his way." In all the fire of her enthusiasm, Abba May put aside such warnings. She had been engaged to a distant cousin, an affair which had ended unhappily and had deeply hurt her. Then she had met this man, who was visiting her brother; she had been taken with him as instantaneously as he had been taken with her, and she had discovered that this was the real love of which the other had been an

4

empty imitation. She understood Bronson Alcott; she knew that he needed somebody to take care of him, as he furthered his great ideas. Joyfully she undertook to be that person, and she continued to be, unquestioning and ungrudging in the outpouring of her strength, until a time came when she taught Louisa to care for him in her place.

A strange, interesting, rather marvelous figure was Bronson Alcott. He was a student, a scholar, and most of all a teacher, to the last depths of his nature. Yet in preparation for these things he had had only the slightest and most irregular of educations, beginning in the farmhouse at Spindle Hill, Wolcott, Connecticut, where he was born, and stretching out over strange roads to come to its end. He used to tell his children how his mother had taught him to write on the kitchen floor. The wide boards were kept covered with clean, white sand in those days, which was swept away at intervals to give place to a new supply. Just before the floor was to be scrubbed, Bronson would be allowed to write in the sand, making the great staggering letters of a little boy just faltering into learning. A — B — cat — dog — patience — fortitude — he moved from the litttle words to the big ones, and presently could read and write. That was as far as his mother could take him; but she was as determined as he

5

that his education should go forward. The rocky ridges of his father's farm were not harder than Bronson's stubborn purpose to learn and to learn in the right way.

The boy's father lacked the money to give his son schooling and, further, lacked totally the inclination to believe in such a necessity. Work was what put a person forward in the world, so he believed, hard work with feet and hands and back. The boy learned to work on the farm; but he was always nursing a greater ambition. As the years passed it became evident that the college education for which he longed was completely out of the question. Therefore he set out to seek what he needed in another way. He was eighteen years old when he started on foot to travel to Virginia and find himself a place to teach; to teach and to study. He had heard that young men of New England were more or less in demand as instructors or tutors in the South. He could see no means of getting there except by walking.

A kindly ship captain gave him a lift by water from New Haven to Norfolk on the understanding that Bronson should repay the passage money as soon as he found work. So anxious was the boy to be rid of the debt that he did not take time to look for a school and closed with the first employment which offered — service with a tinsmith in Norfolk. Part of his duty was to go about the town selling the cups and kettles

6

and pans made by the man who had hired him. He unexpectedly found himself to be a good salesman and rather liked his new pursuit. He repaid Captain Sperry at once and then set out from Norfolk into the country to look for a school.

He found the search most disheartening. Not only were schools scarce and very few of them without a schoolmaster, but the very nature of them was not what he had expected. Rude cabins with chinks in the walls, set at the edge of waste forest land where razor-backed hogs ran wild: such were for the most part the institutions of learning which he came across. Long-legged, shock-headed boys looked dully up from their slates to stare with sullen hostility at the newcomer from Connecticut. The committeemen who had in charge the hiring of teachers seemed little more receptive.

After many miles of tramping, Bronson decided that there was no chance of teaching and returned to Norfolk to his former employer in the tin trade. That worthy man, seeing that he had found a successful salesman, sent him this time into the country to dispose of more of his wares. So well did Bronson carry out his mission that presently he decided to follow this combination of travel and selling on his own account.

"I mean to make peddling in Virginia as respectable as any other trade," he declared stoutly, in a letter to his father. He made it something not merely respectable but alluring. In those days of bad roads and small transportation, the big plantations, far from even the small resources of the village shops, depended on traveling peddlers to renew their supplies of buttons and thread, of ribbons and tin plates and tortoise-shell combs.

It was also true that life in the country in the early 1800's could be very monotonous, so that any person from the outside world, bringing news and opinions as well as material wares, was very welcome. It was surprising to see this upstanding blue-eyed youth from Connecticut, with his neat clothes and quiet manners, come to the door attended by a flock of small slave children and the miscellaneous gathering of hound and mastiff dogs which were supposed to guard the gates against strangers. The mistress of the house would be called and would fall into conversation with the young man. The young ladies would flutter in the background and presently slip forward to look at ribbons and combs and to have a word with him also.

Bronson had a charm beyond the mere possession of good manners, which seemed to capture everyone. Presently the master would come out of his office, from amongst his guns and fishing rods and dog-eared plantation books, and ask whether the pack contained razors or tobacco. He too would fall into conversation with Bronson, which always ended by his being invited to dinner, to pass the night, to spend several days.

After the girls had their evening of talk with him, finding him an interesting, responsive person who could tell them much of what they wanted to know about what was going forward in Norfolk or Richmond, they would retire and Bronson and his host would sit late in the library talking of the great questions of the day.

Young as he was, the boy was wise enough not to discuss slavery; but there were politics and commerce — the exiled Napoleon imprisoned on St. Helena, the recent invention by Fulton of a boat which would run by steam — a world of matters to review as the hours passed. Bronson Alcott was always a singularly good talker, a stimulating talker, who seemed to make other people have better thoughts than they ever had in their own company.

The invitation to stay, if accepted, led to his spending long hours in those plantation libraries, rich with the treasures of three generations. They were enchanted ground to him, for never before had he been within reach of a real supply of books of this sort. History, philosophy, poetry—he plunged deep into them all, trying to absorb as much as was humanly possible before he shouldered his pack and went on again.

After this feast of learning, he had what is another priceless necessity—long, quiet hours in which to think over and appraise what he had read. He tramped the roads alone, sat under the hedgerows and ate his solitary lunch, exchanged brief greetings with the travelers he passed, but always went on thinking, thinking. Very few are the courses in education which allow time to think; but this education of Bronson's was complete, even to that final need.

He saw the big, pillared plantation houses, the squat, whitewashed cabins which housed the slaves; he saw the teams of mules go by jingling with bells, the driver riding the "nigh leader" and guiding the whole four or six with a single rein. He saw the wide cotton fields and the Negroes working and singing, warmed, if it were chilly, by a huge fire of stumps around which they would gather, between the rounds of toting baskets on their heads up to the cotton shed.

He made money and prospered, then grew extravagant and spent the whole proceeds of a single season on new clothes in which to go home. He set out again, prospered once more and finally fell very ill with fever and ague and was nursed back to thin, weak-kneed life by some hospitable Quakers in Norfolk. His strict,

New England belief had been shocked by the lack of religious interest amongst the planters; it was comforted and satisfied by the quiet righteousness of the Quakers. He came home at last, penniless, but so full of memories and experience that the four years amply repaid all of the toil which he had put into them.

When he was a small boy, only newly a master of reading, someone had lent him a copy of *Pilgrim's Progress.* The book fired his spirit and imagination in a way beyond the power of words to describe. He loved it with intense devotion all of his life and made it a fundamental part of his children's education. He once said that the sort of life which would satisfy him completely was to walk through the world all of his days, stopping to have conversations with people by the way. It was just such a life as he had in these years. He received much, but it is very certain that he gave much also, and that the thoughts and ideas he left behind him lived long amongst all of those whom he met.

Although Bronson had not been able to find any teaching to do, except now and then a few weeks of carrying on a writing school in one or another of the larger towns, he came back from his wanderings knowing that he must be a schoolmaster. He understood people, and most of all he understood children; he must teach them.

He became an instructor in a district school in Cheshire. There he met the Reverend Samuel May and through him, his sister, Abba May, who presently, as has been said, very willingly and happily became Abba May Alcott. He left the Cheshire school and began teaching in Boston, where his new ideas came finally to the notice of Reuben Haines, of Germantown.

Schools were not everywhere so rude and rough as those which Bronson had seen in the South; but they were in many places very little better. The able Mr. Haines, enterprising member of the Quaker community outside Philadelphia, who was interested in stock breeding and the stars, in horticulture and the science of the weather, was also greatly interested in education. It was his plan to start a series of schools in his town, to support them from his own funds, and to offer children of all ages the stuff which their growing minds really needed. He journeyed to Boston, saw this young schoolmaster of whom people were begining to talk, and decided that here was the man to give what children wanted. He was right.

Thus it came about that Bronson and Abba Alcott, newly married, came to Germantown to live under the strong protection of Reuben Haines. All their lives the members of this haphazard family were singularly lucky in friends, in people who appreciated and loved them and would do anything in the world for them. Reuben Haines was one of the first and perhaps one of the most interesting of all of these kindly spirits. (Although Bronson Alcott was unfortunate in never being understood by the many, he was singularly blessed in being understood by the distinguished few.)

A tall man, with a thin, thoughtful face, ruddy skin, deep-set, affectionate eyes, and a broad, gentle mouth, such was Reuben Haines. His Quaker plainness of speech and thought, his sturdy directness of high purpose made him an ideal person with whom to work. Under his patronage the school opened in the "Little Paradise" of Pine Place, the house he had bought for Bronson Alcott. All the Quakers of the community liked Bronson's gentle methods; the Germans liked his thoroughness; the children loved him.

It was a cruel mischance for all concerned that the dearly loved Reuben Haines died not long after the founding of the school. Yet in spite of that, Abba and Bronson Alcott had two years at Germantown, the first at least being one of untroubled and prosperous serenity. Here Anna, the eldest child, was born three months after their arrival. And here on November 29, 1832, Louisa also joined them.

It is of course practically impossible that Louisa could have remembered anything of what went on in Germantown, but as is always the case, what she really recollected became inseparably joined to what she heard from other people, so that the memory of these early years always seemed to be hers. The heavy sorrow which hung over her family during her early babyhood was the loss of Reuben Haines, who had died before she was born. The depth of personal bereavement concealed from the eyes of Abba and Bronson for a little while the fact that with his going the school could not longer continue. They struggled forward bravely; but without his backing and without his management the experiment was impossible. It was this anxiety, slowly growing greater, which weighed down that courageous young mother during the months in which lively young Louisa learned to creep, to walk, and then to run.

The friendship with the Haines family, celebrated almost on Louisa's actual birthday by the impromptu reception of all the small Haineses in the Pine Place nursery, was to continue even though the head of the household was gone. The big house, a mile away on the beautiful old farm of Wyck, old even in that day, was still a place of stimulating and happy intercourse* for the

* Visiting.

14

two families. The pair of mothers exchanged advice on their many perplexities — gentle Jane Haines struggling to care for seven children who had no father; and Abba Alcott, in doubt what to do with an unquenchable baby who never would stay where she was put and who, as soon as she could really walk, loved nothing so much as to run away.

Wyck, however, was a place from which even enterprising Louisa never sought to depart. The farm with its ducks and pigs and heavy, gentle-eyed cows was a joy to her; for from the beginning she loved animals and living things. The garden in summer with its tall rows of damask roses, its magnolia trees, its neat round beds with hedges of spriggy boxwood, was such a region as not many young persons have for the practice of their first attempts at walking. Louisa, fat and agile and overflowing with chuckles, had many a glorious hour in that beautiful garden at Wyck.

The family in that plain, stately house, the cheery Haines household, meant more to the Alcotts, more to the memory which they were to carry away from Germantown, than could any of the charms of the farm and garden. There is something in Quaker family life that is not matched anywhere else. In those times, Quakers were cut off from the more usual outside pleasures of living — from music, which had no place in the Quaker scheme of things, from dancing and theaters and gaiety of the social sort. So something very different developed within those big, lively households. The amusement was all from within, a common spirit of delight in small things, of family jokes and understandings, of complete comradeship between parents and children. The utter simplicity, almost bareness of living, did away with the cares and complications which luxuries bring with them. There was comfort in the Haines house — warm fires, good food, spotless cleanliness — but there was never the smallest pretense of anything more.

The deep, square windows had no curtains, but through them the sunshine came flooding in upon the painted floors. The "great room" of the house was merely a hallway, with broad glass doors at each end, and with a glimpse of the peonies and larkspur of the garden massed beyond. Here, only a very few years before, Lafayette had received the worthies of Germantown, the throng of people pouring in at one of the great doors, and out at the other into the garden. Here Audubon had come to give drawing lessons to the eldest Haines daughter; here had come Rembrandt Peale, one of the greatest of American painters, to make a portrait of Reuben Haines, who had befriended him when he was struggling and unknown. And here, most of all, was the unruffled peace and the genuine happiness of living, of a household devoted and gay, high-spirited and happy, even in the face of sorrow. It seems as though the Alcotts' own family life always carried with it the indelible stamp of that earliest friendship. They also always seemed to possess that contentment with simple things, that knowledge of what was the best in living, with which the household of Wyck was so peculiarly blessed.

By the second summer in which Louisa played amongst the ducks and roses, she was a strong and energetic little girl, scarcely a baby anymore. Her eyes were bright and observant, her voice resounding, her will strong. Her mother's busy hands were busier than ever with this lively person to care for. The household at Pine Place held boarding-school scholars as well as the little Alcotts; and there were no servants now, for the school was in desperate straits for money. Without the backing of Reuben Haines, the criticism which always attends a new venture became greater and greater, and the number of scholars shrunk daily. Still the enterprise went forward, no one admitting aloud that it might end in failure. Louisa's very energy and unquenchable restlessness were a distraction for her mother's anxious mind. It was a constant task merely to watch over her and see that she came to no harm.

The two little girls, at least, were very happy as those last spring months at Germantown went by. There were walks along the wooded Wissahickon River, and the Schuylkill, where the wild flowers grew so thickly on the steep slopes, and where the scattering row of great Tory mansions crowned the hill. There was beautiful country everywhere about tidy, well-kept Germantown, with fields blue with violets, with gray-trunked beech trees in the woods and Mayflowers creeping through the brown leaves. There were full, singing streams which ran under arched, stone bridges; there were birds everywhere.

Anna and Louisa could not know how, all those days, their father and mother were so sorely missing that good friend Reuben Haines, missing his generosity, his far vision, and his patient good sense in those small, practical matters of which Bronson had little knowledge. It required more than a gift for teaching at that time to keep alive an undertaking of the nature of Bronson's school. It needed money from some other source than the small fees which could be paid for the pupils. It needed, also, the confidence and peace of mind which comes from a consciousness of security. None of these things did Abba and Bronson have. They did wonderfully well to battle forward as long as they did. The school grew smaller and smaller; it finally came to an end and a great plan dwindled into nothingness.

There was a brief session in Philadelphia at another school which also failed to prosper. Then, suddenly, there was a momentous decision and a great bustle of packing. Without in the least knowing or caring how it came about, Louisa found herself on board a steamer journeying down the broad Delaware River and out into the bay on the way to Boston. It was summer, the shores were green. The old stone farmhouses and cottages showed between the trees, with drifts of bright color in the gardens, to remind the travelers for the last time of the warm, sweet, rose garden of Wyck. They were leaving behind some very good friends, some very happy memories as they sailed away, full of hope for new things.

Not long after the voyage began, Louisa disappeared completely and was not recovered until a thorough search of the whole boat had been made. She was in the engine room, a wonderful place for smells, for glimpses of enormous, glowing fires, of shiny surfaces, and of great steel shafts going back and forth as though by magic. She was covered with coal dust and black grease when discovered, but she had spent an hour of complete happiness. Her mother saw that no such excursion into the lower regions happened again, and must have breathed a sigh of relief when the boat came steaming up Boston Harbor.

The city in which Louisa had been born was broad and low. This new city was upon a hill, with its spires and pointed roofs and the dome of the State House high above her, against the blue of the sky. The steamer puffed and churned the water, backed and roared as it came into its berth. Louisa and her family had arrived at their second abiding place.

She was to learn to know that tall hill very well, although from a different aspect. Bronson Alcott proceeded at once to open a new school, in the Masonic Temple where the plain, large room was as full of sunlight as of beautiful things. He had for assistant Miss Elizabeth Peabody, who later did so much to make a beginning of kindergarten teaching in America. She was a young woman then, still learning, and learning very much from Bronson Alcott. Anna was old enough to be a pupil at the school, and during the long, autumn mornings while she and her father were absent, Abba would walk with Louisa from their house on Front Street over to the Common.

Here Louisa played on the grass, made friends

with the passersby, or, plumping down to rest,
would sit looking up at the tall elms with their
high trunks and enormously long branches, so
different from the round leafy beeches of the
woods at her birthplace. The tall elderly houses
of Beacon Hill looked down on her out of their
many-paned windows, where the blue and pur-
ple glass was a sign of exceedingly aristocratic
old age.

Along Beacon Street there toiled by on the
rough pavement an endless procession of market
carts, of creaking wagons, and those shiny, low-
hung carriages which, a little later, were to be
named Victorias. In them sat beautiful ladies,
overflowing the seats with billowing skirts and
carrying the most minute of parasols to protect
their complexions from the sun.

Sellers of fruit, of pies, of strawberries went
by, calling their street cries to attract customers.
A scissors grinder would move slowly along, his
grindstone on his back, his jingling bell in his
hand, ringing as he walked. Now and then the
town crier would stride past, ringing his bigger,
deeper bell and proclaiming some piece of news
small or great: the dropping of a purse, a warning against pickpockets, the tidings of President
Jackson's newest proclamation. It was all wonderful and exciting to the little girl, so extraordinarily different from the still, rose-bowered

21

garden in Germantown, and the view over green rolling hills.

There was one day when her mother was busy, perhaps away for an hour or two, teaching at Bronson's school, where she had taken charge of the music. Small Louisa set out to see something of Boston on her own account. It is the general experience of newcomers to Boston to begin by losing themselves. Louisa was no exception. She wandered from one narrow street to another, lightheartedly ignoring the fact that she must remember how to come home again. She played with some very ragged children, to their great delight and her own. She caressed passing alley cats; she smiled gaily at strangers; she rambled here and there and finally grew very weary. Some other child would have fallen into panic on finding that she wanted to go home and that she did not know the way. Louisa merely sat down in an entry to rest herself and there fell comfortably asleep with her head on the shoulder of a big, friendly dog. It was twilight when she awoke, but even that did not seem to dismay her. Not far away a great booming voice was coming through the dusk, and a bell was ringing. The town crier was proclaiming:

"Lost, a little girl in a pink dress and green morocco shoes."

Of whom could he be talking, Louisa wondered, as she heard him go through the recital, and then had a sudden inkling of the truth. This magnificent officer of the City of Boston was talking about her. Not in the least overcome, she lifted her small voice and called through the evening darkness:

"That's me."

The Common was always her favorite haunt; there was so much to see there, and so much to do. The Frog Pond, with the tall trees beside it mirrored in the calm water, was an unending joy to her. With such a very lively young person, it was not always possible to hold her firmly by the hand when she and her mother passed near the margin of that inviting pool. There came, as it always does in the history even of the most carefully watched children, the moment when her mother's attention was turned elsewhere for the single, critical moment. Louisa, her own mistress for a brief second, made for the alluring water. She ran to the margin, stood too close, slipped, and went plunging in. There was the shock of cold water, a moment of delighted splashing, a sudden surprised sensation of helplessness, of knowledge that the water was deep, over her head, and that she was strangling and choking. She went down, gasping and fighting, with even in her small mind the instinctive and terrible knowledge that she was drowning.

# CHAPTER TWO

☙ ☙ ☙

# Boston Common

CONTINUOUS MEMORY BEGAN FOR LOUISA, SO
it seems, with that breathless moment of struggling in the Frog Pond. It might very easily have
been her last experience; it has turned out to be
the first in that chain of recollection which
makes up the record of a lifetime. It was a moment which she was never to forget, the choking and sinking, then the sudden apparition of a
face above her, a totally strange, dark face, accompanied by the clutch of strong arms. A minute later and adventurous Louisa was gasping
upon the bank safe and unharmed save for the
quarts of Frog Pond water which she had swallowed.

A young Negro boy had seen the mischance
and sped to the rescue, quicker than any other
of the horrified onlookers. He plunged in,
brought Louisa safe to shore, and, it must be,
slipped away without waiting to be thanked or to
give his name. Although she spoke of her res-
cuer many times in later life, Louisa never knew

what name to call him. But there had come to her very early a warm, personal encounter with a Negro, over whose people America's greatest internal quarrel was slowly waxing more fierce and deadly. Neither Louisa nor the Negro lad, however, had much knowledge of the seriousness of that matter as they smiled at each other in cheerful, youthful understanding and went their own ways.

Other adventures she had, myriads of them, during those early years in Boston; for the crooked streets were full of sunshine, or of beckoning east winds, and it was her impulse to follow wherever desire led her. Very slowly, however, she learned that such escapades were unbearably hard upon her busy mother and that there was a certain element of wickedness in the pleasant act of straying out into the world and forgetting to come home. She tried very hard not to be wicked, did Louisa, but not always with success. Once she put down a list of faults, making it so painstakingly complete that the last item was, "Love of cats." She had inherited a stiff conscience from her New England kindred.

Suddenly, to her blinking astonishment, she found that she was no longer officially "the baby," but that there was another round little girl in her mother's arms — Elizabeth, named for the devoted Miss Peabody. It was time for

Louisa to learn to take care of herself. She was well able to, once she set her mind upon it.

Her memories of that period had much to do with spring breezes, grass on the Common, passing butterflies, and friendly cats and puppies. All of her recollections were beginning to be clear and all of a piece, but she was still quite unconscious of the larger things that were going on above her head in the Alcott household. People came and went, people who were later to become distinguished in every walk of life; but she knew little of them. Many important persons came to visit the Temple School which was for a time really famous. She liked to be taken there; she enjoyed the beauty of its tinted walls, the casts of splendid faces and figures, the wonderful copy of *Pilgrim's Progress* sent from England, which lay in state upon the table. The children of the school, her sister Anna among them, were all a little older than she. They looked rather condescendingly upon the small, rowdy Louisa. She did not know yet about sitting quietly in the attentive circle before the teacher and listening to such unexpected talk as the description of how the spirit should unfold, or what was a child's first duty to himself. Kind, capable Miss Peabody would sit by, putting down notes of all that happened every day, although she did not record Louisa's untutored interruptions and bursts of laughter when something happened to tickle her alert fancy.

Sometimes she would be hushed quickly into respectful silence when the august visitors came in. The Temple School was talked of everywhere and attracted the attention of all who were interested in education, or of travelers from abroad who were being shown the sights of Boston. She saw arrive one day a tall, thin, slightly ungainly man, with such an expression upon his face of serene, radiant kindliness that even she was warmed by its sunshine. She was told, though it scarcely caught her straying attention as she played about the floor amongst the legs of the guests whom he had brought, that this was Mr. Ralph Waldo Emerson. He was inviting her father to visit him at his house in Concord.

"You would like Concord," he was saying to Bronson Alcott who, apparently, had never been there.

Louisa was further introduced for the first time to members of her own family who had so far been only names to her. She saw her grandfather, Colonel Joseph May, a forbidding, somewhat irascible, but unendingly generous old gentleman, who had firm views about children and how good and quiet and well-behaved they should be. Louisa's boisterous energy did not always seem to please him completely, but as he frowned down upon her noisiness from his great dignity of height, she understood as well as he did that behind the appearance of disapproval was a warm and proud affection for all of his little granddaughters.

She saw her uncle, Samuel Joseph May, the gentle, true-hearted brother of Abba Alcott. He had known and loved Bronson Alcott even before she had, and all of his life stood by these two throughout their changing adventures. She saw dear Cousin Lizzie Wells, a niece of her mother's, pink-cheeked, pretty even in the eyes of a small child who thought that she must be very old. She was prettier still in later years, when the pink cheeks were still pink and the hair had turned white. Her staunch friendship for the storm-tossed Alcotts remained undimmed through all the years.

It is not quite plain whether Louisa ever really saw the tremendously important Aunt Hancock, who was such a very old lady even when Abba and Bronson were first married. She became a family legend, with a story of her often in request and often told by Bronson to his children. It was called, "How I went to dinner with Aunt Hancock."

She was a great-aunt of Abba May's, this Madame Dorothy Quincy Scott, and she did not go by any such informal title as made use of her

first name. Not Aunt Dorothy — perish the idea
— nor Aunt Scott, but Aunt Hancock, from the
name of her famous first husband. She had married, when very young, that John Hancock
whose bold signature leads the list of the sign-
ers of the Declaration of Independence. She was
a bride when the Revolution was breaking out
and was mistress of the Executive Mansion when
her husband became the first Governor of Massachusetts. A picturesque gentleman John Hancock had been — courageous, extravagant, patriotic, and formidable, a man of great presence,
coming to preside over the Massachusetts Con-
stitutional Convention in a crimson velvet suit
and plumed hat, setting the first strong hand to
the management of a new and turbulent commonwealth. Dorothy was a spirited wife and
upheld the grandeur of her position in good part.
The trials and troubles of launching a new country were not long over when John Hancock died.

His wife married again; but, within the family
at least, the name of James Scott never seemed to
eclipse the first title, and she was always Aunt
Hancock. She lived to a great age and was the
grand figure of the whole family relationship.
When it was reported that her niece, Abba May,
was engaged to marry a schoolmaster, she issued
an impressive summons that the young man
should be brought to dine with her. She liked to

be kind, but to be so in a splendid and autocratic manner.

Joyous, yet perfectly respectful, was Bronson's description of how she received them in great state, sitting in her big chair as though it were a throne. She entertained them with reminiscences of her great days when she was the Governor's lady on Beacon Hill, and dropped hints to Bronson that he should be properly impressed with the nature of the grand alliance he was about to make. As they went out to dinner, she rated the servants for being slow; she announced that she always began dinner with pudding, since she did not like the foolish new fashion of pudding at the end. She carved the great round of beef herself because, "Governor Hancock's wrist was lame and she had fallen into the habit of carving while at the Mansion."

Bronson understood her fully, saw her kindness and sincerity under the abruptness of her imperious manner, dared to differ with her when she issued one ultimatum after another and after a final flurry of argument got up to go, high in the old lady's favor. About his departure, to meet an appointment at his Sunday school, she was rather irascible and said that "the children might all go to Old Nick" before she would allow her dinner to be interrupted; but she finally dismissed him with a forgiving farewell. As has

30

been said, she was of the May connection, and she had well upheld the family saying that "the Mays are peppery." She was high in the nineties even at this time so that it must be that she had died before the Alcotts' return to Boston. Nonetheless she figures in Louisa's history again.

Louisa and her mother used to exchange glances when the household maxim concerning the Mays was repeated. They had both inherited the excitable May temper. The woman, schooled to self-control by the necessities of life, and the little girl, earnestly trying to learn to curb her own impetuous indignations, used to consult together as to how each should solve the same problem. Cheerful Anna and shy, quiet Elizabeth were like the unruffled Alcotts; but Louisa and her mother remained inflammable Mays to the very end.

Time passed and to Louisa it was a complete mystery how it happened that all at once the family was packing its possessions again and going to live in Concord. She understood very vaguely first, that there had been cruel sorrow in that gay little household, that her mother's heart had been wrung with the pain over the baby brother who came and went away again. Abba Alcott had at certain times a will of iron to hold in her feelings. Only long after, when her daughter saw some of her mother's letters and read in her journal of the despairing cry of bitter grief, did Louisa have any real knowledge of what her mother had suffered over the little boy who was lost, and of whom the girls were taught to speak as though they had really had and known their brother. Elizabeth continued to be the baby of the family, a gentle, cheerful soul, putting to shame the stormy, never-quiet Louisa, who found it so hard to be obedient.

None of the little girls could know how the Temple School was hailed at first with approval and enthusiasm on every side, and then criticized and condemned until it declined slowly to its final fall. Five years it continued, from the time that Louisa was two years old until she was seven. She was old enough then to understand something of what Abolition was, the great question of the time. She heard with uncomprehending excitement how her father's great friend, William Lloyd Garrison, was dragged through the streets, with a noose around his neck, by the mob which wanted to hang him because of his declarations that the slaves must be set free.

She could not realize, however, that people were whispering amongst themselves how unfit it was that an Abolitionist — her father — should be teaching their children. She could see when she visited the school that the numbers had dwindled; she noticed finally the little Negro girl whom Bronson Alcott had included among the pupils. She was not there on the heartbreaking day when Bronson, deaf to all protests and still insisting that his school must be open to all children alike, saw the indignant parents come in, one after another, and take their children away.

The Temple School was closed. Bronson Alcott never had the heart to attempt the founding of another. All of a sudden, as has been said, the family was moving to Concord with — in Louisa's mind — a vague impression of Mr. Emerson's presiding over the enterprise as its patron and guiding saint.

The Hosmer Cottage, as it is still called, stood at the edge of a broad estate and had a large garden with fields behind it. The river, flowing through flat meadows, was within easy reach of those short, vigorous legs which had found Boston Common much too narrow. Louisa raced like a colt over the slopes, for not since they had left Pennsylvania had she known the freedom of open country. There was a keenness in the wind and a smell of pine woods which she had not known at Germantown. There were no luxuriant, stately gardens here, with the warm rose-scented delights of Wyck. But there were the familiar daisies and Mayflowers, and there was that same glorious pink mountain laurel in the nearby hills, which the older country people spoke of as calico bush.

Bronson worked hard at anything he could find to do in the effort to support his household. He toiled at farm labor, at gardening, and at woodchopping. Most of the people whom he knew owned land, worked on it to a certain extent themselves, and were glad of such help as they got from Bronson Alcott. He knew a great deal about farming; he was interesting to work with, for he was always, so tradition universally agrees, extraordinarily good company. Numbers of people had their own wood lots, where was cut every year their store of winter fuel. Bronson Alcott cut for other people and received in return the privilege of getting his own wood for the cold weather.

We can picture, instead of the expeditions along the Wissahickon, the three little girls going with him into the tall, silent pine groves, playing amongst the dry brown needles, finding Indian pipes and jewel-dotted toadstools, or, tired with vigorous running back and forth, sitting down to watch the white, sweet-smelling chips fly from beneath his steadily swinging ax. They talked gravely of everything they had seen and heard, the scholar-philosopher father, the eagerly inquiring Anna, small gentle Betty, and ever-curious Louisa. Their mother was not apt to go with them for there was a new baby in the cottage now, May, the smallest Alcott of all.

Much of the time the older three were taken care of by their father when their mother was busy or when, as she frankly admitted, she was too tired to be wise or patient with them. Abba was a person of varying moods: excitable, quickly moved, always devoted to them all, but often too harrowingly uneasy concerning the family welfare to be entirely calm. It was Bronson who taught them their letters by a strange series of gymnastics on the parlor floor. I was represented by a tall, prim, dignified pose, combined with strutting proudly across the room, X by spreading the arms and legs all abroad, and S by a fearful contortion supposed to imitate the neck of a goose, accompanied by a goose's hissing.

Life was extremely bare in that little house; they had not even the luxury of a stove, and cooked before the fireplace. It was full of gay spirits, however, flooded by a never-ceasing stream of affectionate family jokes. They were all of them generous to the utmost degree, so that it was by Abba Alcott's consent, as well as by Bronson's and the three girls', that they habitually gave away everything that could, or could not, be spared.

A friend of theirs, coming to stay for a visit, observed that their extremely plain and meager meals were reduced from three a day to two, since they were carrying the third daily to a family in great need. Everyone lived simply then; the Alcotts lived rather more simply than the others, although they would have been the last to consider that they were very poor or to feel sorry for themselves on any such account. Life in Germantown amongst the Quakers had already made it clear to them that simple living was no hardship.

One of the diversions of this time was the weekly pillow fight, which the children were allowed to have just before they went to bed. These battles, which, it was understood, were never to become so furious as to endanger life and limb, were an institution which lasted for many years, part of the Alcott tradition to have a good time, no matter what dangers threatened. The children leaped and ran about in their nightgowns — how a good suit of pajamas would have lent itself to the occasion — and finally subsided, breathless and rosy, ready to say their prayers to their father or mother and drop immediately to sleep.

Louisa, on a certain thrilling occasion, received an invitation to go on a visit to Providence, all by herself, unaccompanied by supervising parents. Abba Alcott must have had some misgivings over sending such a lively little girl to stay with kind but unsuspecting elders. She evidently concluded finally that both sides might learn something from the experience and she let Louisa go. There were no other children in the house; but nonetheless young Louisa had a glorious time for a few days, playing with the pet animals, inspecting the spice mill, and being made much of by everyone in the family. Small as she was, she did observe that the grown-up members of the household began to seem a little worn, while she herself became suddenly desperately bored and very homesick. She was finally left to her own devices with the inevitable result that she got into trouble.

In a very short time, she found some dirty children who seemed to her ideal playmates, after the stiff adult companions who had been trying so hard to amuse her. She played with her new friends for a long time in the barn. Finding that they were poorly fed and hungry, she ran in haste to the pantry, by chance unguarded at that moment, and helped herself to figs for them and cakes. She made several journeys back and forth and then suddenly was discovered. Her exhausted hostess could endure no more, gave Louisa a tremendous scolding, and sent her up to the attic to think over her outrageous be-

havior. Poor little Louisa! She had not the faintest idea that in "feeding the poor" she was doing
anything other than what was right. They always
fed the poor at her house, no matter how little
there was with which to feed anybody. She sat
on a trunk, not crying, but thinking dark hard
thoughts, furious with anger, bewildered,
ashamed, knowing that she was disgraced but
not understanding why.

"She meant it kindly, so I wouldn't mind,
Fanny," she heard a voice say outside the door.
There came in one of the young men of the
family, Christopher, who had been so good to
her ever since she came. He said a very little in
brief explanation to make Louisa see that she
had done wrong in taking things without per-
mission, and then he held her on his knee while
she leaned her face against his shoulder and
broke into a storm of weeping. He did not make
stupid attempts to comfort her, but let her cry
her fill, until in sheer exhaustion she went to
sleep. She awoke an hour afterward, frightened
for an instant to find herself in the twilight of
the big garret, then reassured to discover that
she was still upon his knee, within the circle of
his comforting arm. He took her downstairs,
where everything was cheerfully explained and
a promise was given that the family in Concord
need not be told until Louisa herself should give

an account of the affair. That good, wise Christopher she remembered long with infinite gratitude.

At home in Concord, she spent much time playing with a boy named Cy — his last name lost to history. He was always leading her into the most complicated scrapes and she was always willing to be led. He had only to whisper into her ear:

"You darsn't do that," for her to become fired with the feeling that she must do it or die.

She jumped off a high beam in his barn and was borne home on a board, with both ankles badly sprained. He got her to rub red peppers into her eyes, "to see how it felt." He had to guide her home, howling, since little girls with red peppers in their eyes cannot see and are forced to roar with pain.

The first winter passed and with the spring there arrived a new plan. The girls' father, it seemed, was going to England. People there had understood Bronson's ideas on education, had named a school after him, and had invited him to come to see it. There was a bustle of preparation, Anna and Louisa being at last old enough to help. Bronson Alcott was the sort of man who never knew where his socks were, or even his money, but was only conscious of where his books were to be found. Mr. Emerson seemed to have done something to make this possible also. He and Abba both knew that the journey and the acclaim of those who believed in him would comfort Bronson after the bitter disappointment concerning the Temple School. Whatever was Bronson Alcott's dream of what was to result from the journey to England is not quite certain; but it is clear that the hopes of all of them were soaring high when he sailed away and left such emptiness in the little household remaining behind.

It was the girls' mother who taught them now, and who read aloud to them from Dickens and from the shabby old *Pilgrim's Progress* which their father loved so much. The big beautiful copy had been sold, with everything else belonging to the Temple School, to pay a part of its debts. The rest of the indebtedness still hung like a cloud over the little family. Four children and no income make a terrifying problem for a young mother to face. Abba Alcott attacked it bravely, but even the two older girls were beginning to understand that things were in a perilous state. They looked forward as intensely as she did to the day when their father should come home. Surely this journey was going to open some new chance for work and make things easier and safer for them all!

His letters were interesting and stimulating, even to the children. He had met Robert Owen, the leader of a new movement. He met Thomas Carlyle, the most eminent man of his day in England, looked up to as a great writer and a great thinker. Carlyle did not believe in the changes which Robert Owen and Bronson Alcott were advocating and Bronson quarreled with him. That was something of an event; for mild Bronson quarreled with very few in all the course of his life.

It was a great moment when toward the end of the summer the girls heard that their father was coming home. It would be in a month now, then a week, then it was the actual day. Their vague, bright hopes would have some fulfillment at last. Anna and Louisa still did not know what it was that they looked for; they did not observe that, as the days of waiting passed, their mother was looking even more anxious than ever. They were watching at the door for their father, there was a stir of arrival, he was there.

But — they had not been prepared for this! With him were two other men and a boy, a lad bigger than Anna, staring at them as awkwardly as they stared in return. This was Mr. Charles Lane, they were told, the boy was William Lane, and the other man Mr. Henry Wright, all from England. Very slowly it began to be plain to

41

them. The new arrivals were to live with them in the cottage for the winter at least. When spring came they were all to move again; they were to begin a new life, absolutely different from anything that they had known or that anybody had ever tried before.

Louisa was ten now and Anna eleven. They were quite large enough to take in the excitement, the wonder, and also a few of the misgivings that went with this dazzling plan. They could see their mother's face clouded with the thought of how this family was to live, five children and four elders, a total of nine, in a small house large enough, really, for only three or four. There had been so little money for food before — how could it be enough now? The girls understood this as well as she, but, just as she did, they loved their father and wanted above everything else to see him happy. They could not interrupt his delighted talk about the new plan of Transcendentalism — the life in which honesty, sincerity, unselfishness, and all things of the spirit were to be the rule instead of things of the body. The girls did not understand it very well; they half knew that their mother did not believe in it. But, like her, they would follow anywhere that their beloved father chose to lead.

It was a hard winter. The Englishmen were welcomed in Concord, while people talked everywhere of the new plan. Bronson went about in a delighted dream of hopefulness. Abba made little comment, but taught the girls how to help her more and more at tasks to which they brought all the willingness of devoted love. Louisa was not fond of housework and cooking, of helping with the washing, of carrying the water pitchers, and sweeping behind the doors. She was impatient and rebellious and in fact much too young for any such hard labor. But she did it all without much need of being urged, for she was bound that her mother should not be too heavily burdened. Anna was quicker and more skillful and managed her work much more easily. She had a natural gift for household accomplishments, where Louisa had only clumsy energy and an unbounded generosity for doing her part. They had lessons every day with their father.

Even though their food was not much more than fruit, vegetables, and grain porridge, it was hard to supply that household. Abba was adamant on one subject: the rapidly growing children should have milk enough to make them strong and there should be fuel sufficient to keep them decently warm. A baby could not stand the harsh winters of New England without some tender care. There are several versions of the tale about the load of wood; perhaps, indeed, there were several such episodes. This is one of the stories that are told.

There was one night when a windy snow was flying about the little house and the cold was creeping in at every draughty crack. There was practically no wood in the shed and Abba was frantic. Suddenly, quite unannounced, a load of wood arrived, sent by a kindly neighbor out of his own store, got on his own wood lot, perhaps even cut by Bronson himself. The Alcotts' friends had all been anxious over the state of affairs at the Hosmer Cottage and each wanted to do something to help. It was surely a godsend and rejoiced Abba's anxious heart — for a few hours. Later in the evening, with cold and dark and wind still surrounding them, Bronson came in smiling delightedly. A very poor man had just come to him, telling of a cold house, a sick baby, and an empty shed with no fuel. It was so fortunate that they had wood to give him, Bronson told his wife. He had let the poor fellow take all that he needed and had helped him to wheel it home.

But what of his own family, Abba returned, hotly this time, for in spite of her unflinching affection she was not possessed of inexhaustible patience. The Alcotts had a baby too, she reminded him; it was just as cold in their house and would be dangerously so before morning.

Her reproaches were interrupted by a knock at the door. A second neighbor, not knowing what the first had done, had also sent them a load of wood. The fire was piled high again and warmth and cheerfulness filled the house once more.

"I told you that we would not suffer," Bronson reminded Abba. It was his sure belief that God would always provide for those who loved Him. Abba believed it also, with a difference. She thought that God expected people to help themselves as far as they could and not to lay the whole burden upon Him. Through all their lives, Anna and her father tended to accept the first, trusting belief; Louisa and her mother, the greater responsibility of the second. It made no rift between them, but it shaped their destinies to the end.

Spring came at last. A place had been found near Harvard, Massachusetts, not far from the towns of Ayer and Groton, where a hillside farm and an old empty farmhouse could be acquired as the home of the great experiment. It was a dilapidated dwelling with a huge chimney in the very middle of it, standing on a slope that gave, from the doorway, a broad and inspiring sweep of view. The house had been empty for some years; the steep acres had not lately been tilled. But all that, so Bronson and his comrades asserted, would soon be changed into a green paradise, where peace and happiness and brotherly companionship should make every task easy.

It was June when the final move came about. The flowers were blooming in the cottage garden, and the fields about it were strewn with the white of daisies. Abba, going from room to room over the task of once more packing their possessions, looked all about at this place which had been home even longer than the "Little Paradise" of Germantown. She must leave it and she was ready to go, for she loved Bronson more than she loved mere places of comparative peace and comfort. The four little girls were wild with excitement and were not much assistance in gathering up the clothes, the blankets, the cooking utensils, the books, and the busts of philosophers, each as necessary as the other in equipping the new venture. It was raining as they drove away in the little covered wagon with its single horse.

All day they traveled, jolting and laborious, over rutty roads, up cedar-grown hills, down into bushy little valleys. For most of the journey of twenty miles the rain came down upon them in torrents. It did not quench the hopeful spirits of the philosophers or the wild excitement of the children. Abba, with yellow-haired May in her arms, must have let her mind go back many times to the safe white cottage and the friendly clustered houses of Concord. But Louisa and her father did no such thing. The thoughts of both of them were traveling far ahead of the toiling wagon, roaming farther and farther afield in that broad new world.

They were all, however, drooping with weariness as they came toiling up the last climb over the deep line of wheel tracks; for the house did not stand near any highway. The storm was clearing, leaving the whole valley of the Nashua River visible, and the two mountains, Wachusett and Monadnock, looming through the receding rain. The old curled shingles of the big house were black with wet after the June shower, as were the trunks of the twisted ancient apple trees which grew about the dwelling. On account of the old trees, and the new orchard which they intended to plant, Bronson and his companions had decided to call the place Fruitlands.

# CHAPTER THREE

❧❧ ❧❧ ❧❧

# Running in the Wind

THE ANCIENT RED HOUSE THAT HAD STOOD
silent so long was now suddenly full of life
and bustle where there had been so much of
shadows and silence before. A great adventure
was just beginning, and strange bright hopes
were darting and lifting everywhere, just as the
swallows had so long been darting and soaring
about the eaves and above the great chimney.
Louisa, standing on the doorstone, had only one
feeling about this new place to which they had
so surprisingly come. It would make a glorious
playground.

Those unbroken fields, sloping to the river,
how she was going to run and race across them!
Concord had seemed to give her freedom but it
was nothing to what she would have here. Even
before she left Boston, she had become something of a champion in the way of hoop-rolling,
and at the age of six she could drive her hoop
all the way around the Common without a stop.
In Concord, she had developed that art to so

48

great a height that one day she ran and trundled to the foot of Hardy's Hill, a mile from home, then turned about without stopping and rolled the hoop back again. There were greater feats before her now, however, so that hoop-rolling seemed a very distant and a very tame enterprise alongside of what she would find to do here. She was well grown for a girl of eleven, with legs beginning to be very long, like a colt's, and which felt frisky, as a colt's do. They had always skipped a little, all of themselves, as she walked along. Even after the long day of travel they could have skipped and run but she must go in, for her mother was calling her to supper. The twilight creeping up the valley, the misty vision of the mountains, both were beautiful to watch. But better still was the blaze and crackle of the fire in the huge chimney place. All of the travelers were thoroughly ready for supper of brown bread and roasted potatoes, served on tin plates, since as yet no china had arrived.

Louisa watched her father, thin-faced and clear-eyed, as he sat with the rosy light shining upon his mild countenance. She saw him partaking of his share quietly, solemnly, as though he were under a spell. The very food before him seemed to be a mark of the beginning of the great experiment, the undertaking which, according to his belief, was to make the world a different and a finer place in which to dwell. They were to live the perfect life here and to show others that life could be lived perfectly. He ate as though he were in a dream.

Abba moved here and there, intent only on the fact that they had actually arrived, with bundles and kettles and blankets in confusion all about them. The eyes of the children were falling shut from weariness and from a whole day of driving in the fresh, clean air. The baby — they called May the baby still, although she was actually three years old — was already asleep. Elizabeth, plump and eight, was very nearly so. The big, dark eyes of Anna were drooping. Louisa's, for a little longer, were still wide-awake and alert. Her father got up, put away his plate, and spoke. He was embarking upon one of those earnest conversations which were to be such a great part of the life in this new place, the discussion of all things under the sun. He began a little fable which was to appeal to the small members of the household and yet carry a meaning to everyone there.

Louisa never heard the final message of that tale. The long day in the open air brought its expected end at last, and she was led away, blind with sudden sleepiness, to her bed. The tired mother, who had thought of everything, had managed somehow that there were beds of a sort made up on the floor, into which she could tuck the children just as she had tucked them in the cottage in Concord, which now seemed left so far behind.

As we follow the daily life of this odd company through the weeks and months we may be tempted to think with a smile of the ideas which were the foundation of this new life. We must remember, however, that Bronson and his friends, wise in some ways, mistaken in others, had the courage to find out, by the only possible means, where they were right and where they were wrong. There is only one method of testing a system of living; that is by living it.

The year 1843 was at the end of a period very like that which has become all too familiar to us ninety years later. Long wars involving both Europe and America had brought their slowly arriving results of poverty, unemployment, and bewildered suffering. Something was very wrong with the world, everyone said. Here and there a few were trying to organize totally new schemes of living. So many were tried then that we do not have to try them over again today.*

This company at Fruitlands thought that pri-

* When the author wrote this, over 40 years ago, she could not know that communes would again be tried as a way of life for young people in the 60's and 70's.

vate property was wrong and that everything must be owned in common. They followed the principle that animals must not be killed for men's subsistence and must not even be forced to labor for man. They got up at the first light, bathed in cold water, and ate the same food they had partaken of in Concord: vegetables, bread, fruit, and grain porridge. Breakfast was apt to be hurried and lunch eaten in weary silence; but there was a carefully observed rule that as they dined in the evening there must be talk of higher things. The men wore linen smocks, since wool robbed the sheep and cotton was produced by slave labor. They made their firmest stand of all against slavery.

There was much laughter in the old place, since four growing little girls can make it impossible for even a company of philosophers to be entirely solemn. There was in every corner that bright content that comes to a place when people are happy. All through the summer Louisa spent glorious days, waking when the first red showed above the mountains, and running out into the sparkle of sunshine on dewy fields. As the fresh morning wind would come down from the hills, she would turn so that it was behind her and go racing down the long slopes, feeling so well, so light, and so fleet that it was as though the wind could go no faster than she.

Sometimes she sat in the shadow of a great clump of pines and heard the breezes sing deep-voiced in the branches. She would come in from these excursions, bright-eyed and rosy, to work beside quiet, industrious Anna at the tasks of the house.

Here was all the pleasure and excitement which comes to every young person who spends a summer on a farm. The animals — it was necessary at last to bring in the aid of oxen to break the stubborn hill acres — the miracle of the growing seeds and dark furrows turning green, the black crows flapping overhead, the smell of blueberries with sun on them, the solemn-faced woodchucks sitting upright amongst the stones — all these were a new and continued delight to the girls. Louisa and Anna had the feeling, not merely that this was an alluring life, but that there was the zest of a strange adventure combined with the ordinary round of labor. They understood that the undertaking was unlike anything that had ever happened before and that somehow they, the two girls, had an actual part in it. They carried on their own share of the work in the farmhouse, Anna with a good deal of skill for a girl of twelve, Louisa still eagerly and awkwardly, both of them determined to be of help to their mother.

What they did was an odd mixture of pleasure and toil. Anna could bake bread and she and Louisa could get a meal without older help. Anna would go for a walk in the woods and come home with a shining face, unable to speak of all the beautiful things which she had seen. "My favorite word is 'beautiful,' " she wrote in her diary. Both the elder children would help with the washing and ironing and then would go out to gather blueberries and blackberries in the thickets on the rocky slopes above them. Anna gave lessons to her sisters, but she was also not too old to play fairies with them in the mossy clearings of the pine wood, or to gather oak leaves and flowers to make wreaths for everyone in the household.

At the end of the day both little girls would write in their journals, Anna filling hers with quiet, pleasant reflections and a record of the work she had done, Louisa covering her blotted pages with accounts of her turbulent thoughts, of her glorious runs on the hill with the wind all about her, and, alas, of her quarrels with Anna, of their reconciliations, and of her grief over the bad temper which would not be controlled. She was to find very early and was to know until very late that it is hard to be good. Abba Alcott, tired and hard pressed, did not always know how to calm the sudden storms. Bronson almost always could. No matter what had been the small differences, the day always ended in peace and with an unbroken knowledge between the two girls of how much they loved each other. They went to bed in the little room under the roof, listening to the sounds above, to the wind sliding by overhead or stirring in the tall elm trees, or to the steady rain on the shingles so close above their heads. Louisa was excitable and sometimes was so full of the events of the day that she would lie in the dark, broad awake. She would recite poetry to herself until presently the rhymes and rhythms would mix with the rustling of leaves or the patter of rain and she would be asleep.

They would walk to the mill and watch the water go splashing over the dripping wheel, and see the smooth stream slide quietly over the dam and plunge, white and glittering in the sun, into the pool below. They would help rake the hay and carry it to the waiting cart; they would go up to the wood and build bowers of twigs and ferns for their dolls. On rainy days they would both curl up in the big kitchen and read endlessly. In the evening Bronson would not be too tired to get out the beloved book and read aloud in the light of the bayberry candles, the story of which Louisa spoke in her diary as "dear Pilgrim's Progress." Then at last, when it was bedtime again, he would put down the book, look about with his mild, radiant smile and ask,

"What is God's noblest work?"

They must all answer: the older philosophers, Charles Lane and Abram Wood and Joseph Palmer, and also the children, Anna reflectively, Louisa impulsively, sweet, round little Elizabeth sleepily. Abba Alcott, who had toiled without ceasing for a moment since daylight, would be sitting by the single lamp, sewing as though her life depended upon it. She was the only woman there, and hers was the only really able pair of hands for the tasks of preparing food, sweeping, washing, and keeping all this household clothed. The questions went round from one to another, but she did not answer. It was agreed that she was to be excused, that she had other things of which to think.

Louisa was growing so rapidly that she was beginning not to know what to do with her long arms and legs. She still thought that running on the hill was the most glorious thing in the world, and yet — it was strangely beautiful to sit longer and longer at the edge of the woods, looking down on Fruitlands and wondering — wondering — not as to what was God's noblest work or what was the nature of Man, not about any of the things talked of by the philosophers before the fire, but wondering and wondering still.

There is a certain incident, belonging to Louisa's early years, which it is very difficult to place in regard to time. It made so deep an impression upon her, and she spoke of it so often afterward, that it cannot be omitted from any account of her life, even though there is no record of just when it happened. It shall be told here.

One day as she stood in the kitchen she heard a strange sound in the brick oven. Before cooking stoves came into use and when open fires were still the only means for preparing food, it was usual where there was a large chimney to take the space next to the fire for a bricked-in oven with an iron door. Wonderful cooking was possible in those old ovens; there are indeed certain kinds of bread which cannot be baked successfully in any other way. Louisa knew that no such noise was appropriate to the baking of bread; curiosity possessed her and she opened the door and peeped in. A face looked out at her, a black face, gaunt, and as wild and desperate as a hunted animal's. She jumped back, slammed the door, and ran to her mother.

Abba told her in a whisper that there was a man hidden in the oven: a contraband. Louisa was to say nothing of what she had seen, since even the people in the house who knew of such a presence did not talk of it to one another for fear of being overheard. Contraband was the name given to those runaway slaves who managed to slip away from the plantations of the South and make their way to the freedom which they could win by getting to Canada. People who sympathized were always willing to hide the fugitives and to pass them from one place to another until they came within reach of safety. If they were caught they were carried back to chains and floggings while their benefactors were liable under the law for concealing them.

Few laws have been so often broken. Long before the actual climax of the slavery quarrel, the matter of fugitive slaves was a sore point between the North and the South. When in the white heat of final fury South Carolina led her sister states out of the Union, she declared that the North had been the first to break the original compact by habitually giving shelter to runaway slaves. Abba and Bronson Alcott were amongst that great number who gave aid and shelter to the contrabands and thus aided, by one more instance, the growth of the tremendous quarrel which became the Civil War.

Louisa Alcott spoke several times in the record of her life of that moment when she saw what slavery really was. Her family think that perhaps the incident took place in Germantown, where the house at Pine Place had a big, farmhouse kitchen and a brick oven. The brick oven at Wyck was enormous. It is certain that Reuben

Haines and his Quaker friends were strongly against slavery and that various old houses in the town have hiding places still pointed out as the refuge of runaway slaves. But Louisa was only two when she left Germantown; and she speaks always of the affair as something which she recollected so vividly that it seems scarcely possible it happened when she was so small. It could not have been in Boston and almost surely was not in Concord. Fruitlands was somewhat out of the ordinary line of travel for the escaping contrabands; yet all through New England there are places, as at Germantown, where they have been hidden. We cannot be sure where and when she saw that terrified face in the darkness, but we do know that she never forgot it, and that it helped to bring her to a great resolve in later years. Even when she was only eleven it was about slavery as well as about many other great and small things that she wondered as she sat on the hillside above Fruitlands.

The grain was tall in the sloping fields, growing even more rapidly than young Louisa; the apples were swelling on the trees; summer was passing. So many questions had been asked about the new experiment that the philosophers found themselves too often called from their work to explain their ideas and principles to others. It was beginning to be time for the harvest; everyone was anxious to make sure of the barley which was to be the chief crop of the newly broken fields. What they had to put in the barn for the winter might make for either the life or death of the enterprise. Just as the grain was ripe, however, just after it had been cut and stacked to dry, there came a summons to a conference which Bronson and his friends could not put aside. The barley could wait for a little, they were sure; and here was another harvest which they felt was more pressing.

They trudged away and left Abba, the four girls, and young William Lane to take care of the farm. One day passed calmly, but by the next trouble began to threaten. The merciless warning of a northeast storm was in the sky; dark clouds were rolling up. Wind and lightning showed among the thunderheads; rain was evidently upon them. The children ran out, bringing baskets and bags, anything in which grain could be carried. Abba snatched from the pine chest her Russian linen sheets and ran after the others. The sheets were spread upon the ground; the little crew of harvesters worked like ants; they carried their loads to the barn, then rushed back, panting. The big sheaves almost upset the smaller workers, the grain spilled down their necks, and the stubble was harsh and sharp beneath their running feet. But by the time the storm broke, the bulk of the crop was safe under the big barn roof. There was something, at least, put away for the winter.

There was corn to harvest later, and again the children helped, this time with the husking, which went on into the night, lit by lamps in the barn. It was beginning to grow cold now; searching winds swept down from the highlands and played at will through the draughty old house. The band of philosophers had dwindled; hard work had quenched the enthusiasm of some; cold and discomfort hastened the going of others. Charles Lane and his son would not give up, nor would Bronson Alcott. But he and Lane would have long talks in the little study away from the main room. The girls, passing the door, would hear such unaccustomed words spoken as money, crops, income.

Louisa never knew just when it was that she began to feel the stirring change in the air and realized that a chill cloud of desperate trouble was slowly settling down upon them all. Her father had worked like a dozen men upon the farm, in the relentless determination to make it produce enough to feed them all. He was always tired but it was not weariness which shadowed his countenance now. Abba Alcott's deep eyes followed him wherever he went about the house. She herself was worn to the verge of exhaustion, but she toiled unfalteringly at her daily work. The look on her own strong face was not one of mere anxiety. It was terror.

They had celebrated Elizabeth's birthday in June, in perfect fashion, with a little tree in the woods, decked with presents, with a procession winding up the path, singing as it went, to the music of Charles Lane's violin. William Lane and the girls had lessons with their father and instruction in music from Lane. They shared all the tasks together, the children and Abba sometimes helping to rake hay in the fields, Bronson often doing the cooking, Lane having been known to assist with the washing. It was all very gay at first; then it was gay no longer. Louisa's birthday came and her father's, both on the twenty-ninth of November, but the snowy day was little more than barely noticed as a festival.

"Our way has gone wrong," Bronson was heard to voice his despair at last, as he and his friend sat in the study. Lane, apparently not so much disturbed as his companion, answered in an eager stream of talk, through which one phrase sounded plainly again and again.

"The Shakers, the Shaker Community, has succeeded where we have failed."

Across the river, on the slope of the hill opposite, stood the Shaker village with its plain houses, its spreading orchards, and broad, well-tilled fields. They were a body of people who also owned all property in common and did their work by sharing the tasks. The men lived in one building and the women in another, for they did not believe in marriage and thought there should be no such things as wives and husbands and households with children. The Government turned over to their care the orphans and foundlings which, today, are brought up in state homes. These children lived all together in common nurseries. They had good food and sensible training, but, so Louisa and Anna must have wondered, as they looked at those gray buildings beyond the hill, did they have enough love? Did the babies ever cry for someone to rock them; did the older girls ever long for a person so near and so dear as to be almost a part of oneself—a person like Mother?

Life at Fruitlands was strange and hard, but the little Alcott girls did not know it. So surrounded were they by love and watchfulness that the discomforts and privations which crept more and more into their days did not seem to matter. What did matter was that these two beloved ones who were their whole world were growing day by day more sorrowful and desperate. Often and then oftener, Bronson Alcott and Charles Lane would walk away over the hill to the Shaker village, and Abba Alcott, the girls' mother, would watch them from the window.

One night Louisa, slipping into bed with her

sister, felt Anna's firm body suddenly shaken with sobs. The two clung together, weeping wildly in fully admitted terror.

"What is it?" Louisa questioned desperately.

It was something about Mr. Lane, Anna explained. She had got an inkling of the truth — that Lane thought they ought not to be there, Abba, Anna, Louisa, and the little girls. He was trying to persuade Bronson to give them up, to live as the Shakers did, and to forget that he had any children or that they ever were a family.

Louisa's heart stood still at the very thought. Few children loved their parents and each other as did the little Alcotts. They had so little else; but they at least had one another! Louisa's strong warm nature held passionately to her dreaming father, to her devoted, toil-driven mother, to the two smaller ones, gentle-spirited Elizabeth and May of the vigorous will. She had the feeling that she wanted to protect them as well as to love them. She knew even in her child's mind that her mild visionary father, with his great ideas, needed them all to help him keep safely in the path of ordinary life. Charles Lane might insist that, for the sake of a tremendous purpose, a man ought to give up such small things as family love, loyalty, and devotion to one's own. He did not know that it is upon such things that the very structure of life is built. It was in those dark and desperate days that Louisa learned to know the truth of what family life should be, learned it and never forgot.

Did the support of the "dear Pilgrim's Progress" help them then? I think that it must have, that each one of them thought of that immortal ordeal and gathered some courage from it. There is a glorious passage when Christina, the mother of the family, goes down into the river, without fear or hesitation, to reach the beauty of the life beyond. Abba must have felt that she was crossing some such river of doubt and terror now, must have felt the water very cold about her knees as she girded her fortitude and waited. No discussion of the matter passed between her and the older girls, but they all three understood one another — everything in Louisa's later life shows how fully she understood what was threatening them then.

One thing Bronson Alcott believed, in which he was right seventy years before other people began to see the same truth. He maintained that children had minds and hearts and spirits of their own, and should have a voice in what was decided concerning them. It was a portentous moment in the history of them all when he finally acted upon that belief.

On a certain evening when Charles Lane was temporarily away, Bronson called a family council and laid the matter before them all. He and his wife and the two older girls faced the issue squarely; should they separate for the sake of Bronson's idea or should they keep together? There was no question of what the children thought. Anna and Louisa were able to speak their passionate desire; the smaller ones, feeling vaguely that something was wrong, merely cried and clung to their father. Abba Alcott even now did not say a great deal. He must do what he felt was best, she told him, but he must be sure what was best. He listened with bent head. He could make no decision even now. Next day, Charles Lane came home.

Then suddenly everything was settled. Not the children, perhaps nobody, ever knew just how it came about. Charles Lane and his son were gone, after some scene with Bronson Alcott of which happily there is now no record. In that bare house, with the December blasts whirling about it, the Alcotts all gathered close, fiercely close together before the hearth, safe from being torn asunder.

But something had happened to the children's father. Louisa stared at him as he sat in his chair, looking about at them with a broken smile. He was happy to be with them, but the fearful struggle had shattered him. He was worn out, he was ill unto death. He had worked so desperately on the Fruitlands farm, trying to draw from those unwilling acres a living for his family, for his companions, and his idea! He was tired with this outward struggle; he was still more worn from the battle of doubt within. The children, with round eyes of terror, saw him lying on his bed finally, lying there day after day, too ill to move, to speak, or to eat. It seemed as though after all he was going away from them.

Abba Alcott's unbroken spirit still stood firm in that house as the days passed. From her the girls learned to see that when all else fails courage is the only thing left to cling to, courage and faith in God. The slow days crept by as the illness increased and then spent itself, until rest and untiring care and returning peace of mind began to accomplish their ends. Bronson Alcott was courageous too. He had seen his great experiment fail in spite of everything he dared to put into it. Although he had fallen into some errors, he had been wise enough in the very last hours of despair to know that he was mistaken. He had refused finally to wreck the lives of his beloved ones even though he felt that he had wrecked his own. Strength and health began to come back very slowly, as little by little he was drawn away from the open door of death.

Abba's devoted and understanding brother came to her aid in this desperate situation. He had never failed to appreciate Bronson. Through the help of Samuel May, she was able to rent a house in the nearby town of Still River, a house dignified enough to boast a name of its own: "Brick Ends." As soon as Bronson was sufficiently recovered, they left the draughty, bare farmhouse and moved their few remaining possessions to the village.

It was very different from the gay arrival in June, that day when they set out on the journey away from Fruitlands. Bronson Alcott, still helplessly ill, was carried out of the house and laid wrapped in blankets upon a wood sledge. That was the easiest way to take him over the rough road to Still River. Anna walked beside him, his gentle, unquestioning daughter, who had wondered and suffered over all this incomprehensible affair, but who took it as it came, with no rebellion or protest of her own.

Louisa came behind, one rapid thought treading fast upon the heels of another. How was this strange adventure to end? Where were they going now and what were they to do? They were together at least, and as long as she lived she was going to battle against anything that might try to separate them. People who loved one another must stand together. So far she, who was barely eleven years old, had been able to do little; she had only stood by and watched the peril coming closer. But she could help soon; she must help; she would help always. Her old comrade, the wind, was sweeping and calling all across the hill, but she had no time to turn back for a last run with him. Louisa Alcott, as she trudged away over the snow, had set her face determinedly toward the real adventures of life.

# CHAPTER FOUR

❧❧ ❧❧ ❧❧

# Roderigo's Boots

THE ALCOTT FAMILY WAS MOVING. IT WAS
not the first time, as we well know, nor yet the
last; for, in the first twenty-eight years of Louisa's
life, this household was to achieve the record of
twenty-nine moves. Scars on the mahogany and
walnut dressers bore witness now of perhaps a
dozen upheavals through which they and the
Alcotts had gone together. Louisa, standing on
the threshold and watching the low-posted beds
and the horsehair sofas come staggering in, was
now thirteen years old.

Moving had never ceased to be an adventure
with the casual Alcotts, and, with the exception
of that single heavyhearted departure from
Fruitlands, was invariably a gay occasion. The
rambling brown house which was now to be
their domicile resounded with cheery voices all
along its dark passages. The corridors offered
steps up and steps down, to betray unwary feet
not yet used to the small individualities which
everyone expected in houses of the Revolution-

ary period. No one, however, cared about such small inconveniences. Louisa's spirit thrilled to the adventure of taking up life in a new place, in a storybook old dwelling with a pine-covered hill behind it, and with a gate opening upon the Concord-to-Lexington highroad. Down that road Paul Revere had galloped; over the pine-covered hill had marched a company of redcoats to take part in the first battle of the Revolution. The family was glad to come back to Concord, the peaceful, pleasant town with its square white houses and with its neighbors who were all friends.

Since leaving Fruitlands two years before, they had dwelt, first for eight months in Still River, later for a short time in Concord, taken into the house of a good friend who was glad to help them in their extremity. Finally they moved to Boston, where Abba as well as Bronson looked for work for the support of the family. Now, however, under the suggestion of that unfailing friend, Mr. Emerson, and with his help, they were returning to Concord, this time to reside in a house that actually belonged to them. It seemed as though at last they might be settling upon some permanent plan of living. They decided to name the house Hillside; it is now known as Wayside.

The big, wooden dwelling had been surrounded at first with various buildings, sheds, a wheelwright's shop, and a barn across the way. Mrs. Alcott, with vigorous enterprise, had the barn moved to their side of the road, had the shop cut in two and each half attached to an end of the house. In one of these two small wings was a little room which was to be Louisa's very own, where she could keep all her treasures, write and read, and do whatsoever she liked. It had a door into the garden, so that she could run outside, under the trees, whenever the fancy seized her. How long she had desired just this, a place of her very own!

The house had eight outside doors, so that, as they were settling to the table, or to read about the lamp in the low-ceilinged sitting room, a rap somewhere would send every member of the family flying, each one to a separate door, to admit the arriving friend. It was there, with a great deal of flurry and fluttering, that the household sat down at last, that evening of the moving-in. Anna had been busy in the kitchen; Louisa had kindled crackling fires in the numerous fireplaces. The smaller children were washed, and Bronson came out from the congenial task of unpacking his books. Around the table there began a hilarious account of the adventures of the day, each person having his or her own joke to tell of the absurd mishaps which go with moving, of the things which were lost and broken, of the lack of things which could not be had in a household where money was still as scarce as good spirits were abundant.

In Louisa's eyes the two great assets of the new abode were the little room in the wing and the barn. The Alcotts never kept a horse, although the girls often dreamed of galloping down the shady Concord roads, as did the more fortunate members of their acquaintance. There are, however, a hundred good uses for a roomy barn other than those intended by the original builder. As everyone knows, barns are particularly well suited for dramatic purposes. The drama at that time was Louisa's ruling passion. It is probable that before she slept that night she was already busy outlining plots wherein beautiful heroines were rescued from dungeons, and princesses, disguised as slaves, won the hearts of disillusioned kings. As soon as the little room was in order, very bare and neat, with the scent of dried herbs in the closet, Louisa sat herself down to the table and fell to creating. Thus were born not only Duke Roderigo, but Duke Roderigo's boots.

Some little time later the Alcott's Concord friends were invited to witness the first, and possibly the only, performance of a drama in three acts by Louisa Alcott, enacted, from the hero and the villain down to the page boy who brings in the cup of poison, by the four Alcott girls: stage manager and mistress of costumes, Louisa Alcott. She was good at creative dressmaking and knew just what her characters should wear. The hero was of the extravagantly noble kind, full of splendid motives and manly virtues. It was absolutely impossible to portray him without a slashed doublet, a sash, and tall, romantic boots. Louisa, with her vigorous mixture of fanciful and practical energy, made not only the hero, but the boots as well.

Somewhere she laid hands upon some skins of tanned leather and cut out crude profiles of what she imagined a nobleman's boots to be. These she sewed together, over and over, as a less enterprising young person sews patchwork. The result was truly magnificent. To walk any distance in the boots would have been quite impossible; but noblemen of Louisa's kind did not walk, fortunately; they strode a few paces to the rescue of captive maidens. Louisa trod the boards of the barn theater through her first play in a blaze of glory. The curtain went down to applause which shook the old barn rafters. Some of the acclaim was for Anna, who was a really gifted actress, some of it was for Louisa; and a great deal of it was deservedly for the boots.

Excited and delighted by her first success,

Louisa worked away in the little room, writing more and more dramas of the same sort. So many plots came crowding to her brain that, from plays, she overflowed into stories of the same grandiloquent sort. They were cut out, as the boots had been, by the pattern of what she imagined the life of the high nobility to be, and they were put together with the same industrious ingenuity.

Between the stories and plays she dreamed long dreams of the great things she hoped to do. "Am I going to be an actress," she wondered, "or a playwright, or a story writer?" She had no idea which it was to be.

Whatever it was, she was going to be it with all her might. Yet underneath her soaring fancies there lay a firm foundation of practical resolution. She saw plainly that her father, though recovered now, had very little real knowledge of the jostling world about him, that her mother was worn and worried over the problems of living. She could see that her sister Anna was as ambitious as herself, that Elizabeth was not strong, and that little May was growing up with a beauty-loving nature of passionate intensity. No children ever loved one another and their parents more than did the Alcotts. The way in which Louisa adored them all as the years passed could never be put into words — the way she loved them and intended to take care of them.

There in the little room she made what she called the plan of her life and vowed to herself that she would give these beloved ones what each one needed. There was to be security for her father, peace and comfort and "a sunny room" for her mother, opportunity for Anna, care for Beth, education for May. One of the most interesting tales in the world is the record of how resolutely Louisa kept that promise and how, no matter what things went against her, she always refused to be beaten.

She was not, however, taken up continually with thoughts of the drama and of the future. She still ran in the fields and climbed the hills; she loved to sit under the pine trees on the ridge behind the house and think long, intense thoughts. Through all that first summer at Hillside she was free and happy. She would write busily in the little room undisturbed and would often work late into the evening. When she was tired at last she would put down her pen and run out into the garden. The grass would be dewy and soft under her feet, the tall fruit trees would be dark against the stars. She loved to climb up into the crooked, comfortable branches and sit there dreaming until her thoughts had traveled far away from ordinary things. She would look back within her memory upon Fruit-lands and all that incomprehensible incident which still cast a dark memory over their lives. She would wonder whether it was over and whether they were going to follow an ordinary existence now, to the end of their days. She hoped that they would not.

It is not certain whether she ever knew of the very last act in that curious drama of Fruitlands. Abba Alcott, whose struggle for the safety of her family had been so silent and so desperate, Abba whose will had stood against Charles Lane's and had finally won the day, seems in the end to have regretted her victory. Bronson's illness and despondency lasted so long, his heartfelt sorrow over the failure of the experiment was so great, that at last even his wife's brave determination faltered. She sat down and wrote a letter, such a letter as once she never would have dreamed that she could indite. She wrote to Charles Lane and asked him to come back, asked him to take up work once more with Bronson, so that he might be happy again. She knew what such a thing meant. But she asked Charles Lane to come.

With what agony of anxiety she must have waited for his answer. As has been said, she was a woman of most intense feeling. We know she was, for otherwise she could not have humbled her pride and put by her greatest desire for the sake of her affection for Bronson Alcott. Perhaps not even he knew of her offer; it seems scarcely possible that she told the girls of it. The reply came at last. Charles Lane had not continued with the Shakers, whom he had joined on leaving Fruitlands. Somehow that connection also had been unhappy. He was going back to England. With his departure the shadow of his presence vanished from their lives forever. The Alcotts never saw him again.

One former member of the Fruitlands establishment, Joseph Palmer, came back to buy the abandoned land and to keep up a strange sort of idealized existence on the old place. He vowed that no traveler should ever go away hungry from his door. On one side of the farmhouse hearth stood a great iron pot of beans, on the other a similar one full of potatoes. Anyone was welcome to come in and help himself. Destitute people took refuge there, sometimes staying for months or years. Joseph Palmer and his wife, Nancy, made no profession of being Transcendental philosophers; their only system of thought was a complete overflowing of human kindness. Yet there was nothing weak and vacillating about the character of old Joseph. A farmer near him, Silas Dudley by name, disputed with Palmer the right of way across Dudley's

land from the Fruitlands farm down the highroad.

Mr. Emerson recounted to the Alcotts how,
when a deep snow fell, Joseph Palmer undertook to clear the drifts away from the path across
the disputed land, while Silas, the owner, sally-
ing out with his shovel, fell grimly to work to
shovel it on again. Regardless of the pleas of
their alarmed households, they worked against
each other all day long, two old men in the bitter cold. Finally a compromise was suggested.
If Mr. Emerson were called upon to decide which
was right, would both agree? They said they
would; Emerson's was a name to conjure with,
such was everyone's confidence in his justice and
his impartial friendship. The dispute was decided
and the tale carried home to the Alcotts. Louisa
and her sisters could laugh over it, in spite of
the dark memories of Fruitlands. But it is not
certain whether Abba could join in their
laughter.

What a friend Mr. Emerson was! Always
when things seemed difficult, when troubles
were on the point of overwhelming this happy-
go-lucky family, he was at hand to offer aid.
Advice, belief, more substantial things, he was
ready to give them all. His big, square white
house was not far away, a refuge and meeting
place, for all of his legion of friends. Here in

the parlor, sitting before the broad, white-paneled fireplace, Bronson Alcott could talk and talk of the things deepest in his heart and know that he spoke to one who would truly understand. Those red velvet, cushioned chairs, the long sofa against the wall, the crackling flames shining on Emerson's unclouded face, what a scene of peace it was for a storm-tossed philosopher! Sometimes there sat with them a very shy, young man who did not say much, but whose ideas were like clear flame when once he gave voice to them. Henry Thoreau, so diffident that very few people ever could say they really knew him, was a warm and close friend of the Alcott and Emerson families. What talk it was, there by the fire, of the threat of war still a great way off, of the new ideas, of Transcendentalism, of regrets and wondering over Fruitlands. Fiery talk, quieted by Emerson, gloomy talk, cheered by him! Wonderful talk that will not easily be matched in our hurried time!

For Abba Alcott, Mr. Emerson had practical, steadying counsel, shrewd advice concerning those money matters which perplexed her so sorely. To Louisa he gave the freedom of his library and all that went with such a privilege. She was at liberty to choose anything from those tall mahogany shelves which reached to the ceiling, to curl herself in a corner of the comfortable sofa and read to her heart's content. Her curiously varied education, got partly through her father, and a great deal of it through reading by herself, received a strong impetus here where such a wealth of wise, friendly books was ready to her hand. She could read anything she wished; but she got advice now and then, suggestions dropped gently by the owner of that hospitable library. She would slip in, see Mr. Emerson sitting at work, writing busily on a board upon his knee, for he never even owned a desk. She would take down a volume, get a quick smile from that strong, sensible, infinitely friendly face, and slip quietly out again. She would stop in one or another of the other rooms, the broad, sunny dining room, or the shabby, beloved parlor where the chairs and the carpet were so worn by the coming and going of philosophic feet. She might perhaps peep into the guest chamber, the room of honor opening from the dining room, which the Emersons, also fond of *Pilgrim's Progress*, called "The Room Looking to the East." Its windows opened upon fields and stone walls, upon rows of apple trees along the road which wound up the hill and disappeared. Matthew Arnold slept there as did many another distinguished guest who came from afar to seek out Ralph Waldo Emerson.

It was no wonder that Louisa, just growing

into the romantic age, acting extravagant dramas and composing them, reading the great tales of romance, should have plunged herself into the very depths of fathomless sentiment. She found in Mr. Emerson's library a book which told of a little girl's adoring admiration for the great poet, Goethe. She made up her mind at once that she would be like Bettine, and that Mr. Emerson would be just the proper subject for such hero-worship. Little by little, she built up a dream of romantic feeling about this dear friend of them all. When she had been writing late in the little room she would, as has been said, slip out into the darkness of the garden, climb into the friendly arms of one of the big, hospitable cherry trees, and sit there watching the moon come up over the dark hills, thinking deeply romantic thoughts. Louisa was growing up. That she was not quite grown and still a little girl, we know from the fact that the owls, swooping silently through the still night, would frighten her so much that she would run headlong into the house to bed.

She left flowers very shyly on the doorstep of her adored Mr. Emerson. She sang a serenade under his window, sang it in German and in such a small voice that nobody heard her. The object of her devotion was utterly unconscious of what was going on in her youthful heart. Years later, when Louisa was so well grown up that all this seemed like a past existence, she told their friend of the period of sentimentality concerning him, and the two laughed together over the intensity of her young feelings. She had written him letters which she never delivered. He asked for them when he heard of them so long afterward; but he was not allowed to see them. It was probably Louisa's first act when she came to years of discretion to destroy those missives; for when Mr. Emerson finally heard of them they had long since been burned.

In the barn were held meetings of an important organization, the Pickwick Club. Only the Alcott girls were members; but they published a paper just the same, with laboriously written numbers full of stories by all of them, sentimental tales of Anna's, dashing poems by Louisa. The sisters also maintained a post office on the hill behind the house, where a girl friend of theirs would leave her letters, flowers, and books, and where the Alcotts would post their replies. The post office was a well-loved institution which lasted as long as they lived at Hillside.

Thus passed the first summer. There was a day in the autumn when Louisa had gone out for an early run and stood at the summit of a wooded ridge to watch the day break above the river. The maples were scarlet and the birch trees gold all about her; the morning was absolutely still, there was a thin mist over the low meadows beyond which the sun was coming up. It was a moment of such complete and unbelievable beauty that it made her suddenly feel that she was transformed into a different person. She said afterward that she never understood God so fully as she did at that second, and that she understood Him forever after, from having realized all at once the beauty of the world which He had given her to dwell in. She went home with something new in her heart which she was never to lose.

From the spring that she was thirteen until the autumn of the year that she was sixteen years old, she lived at Hillside. Not much seemed to happen to her; and yet, those years were extraordinarily important in what she learned, in what she discovered, and in what friends she made. There is no doubt that they were the happiest years of her life.

For the first time she went to school, the winter that she turned fourteen. Louisa and Anna had much ado to persuade their father and mother to let them go; for it had been Bronson's pride that, although he had no other pupils now, he could at least undertake the education of his daughters. He and Abba were wise enough to see, nevertheless, that the girls needed companions of their own age and should not always study alone. Anna found the new life interesting and easy to get used to; but it was not so simple for Louisa. She was very shy and was now so tall as to be conspicuous amongst girls of her own age. She was awkwardly conscious of being oversized and always felt large and clumsy and unduly burdened with hands and feet. She was so gay and so full of good spirits, however, that she was immediately welcomed by her new comrades. As they all grew better acquainted, some of them were surprised and startled by the sudden changes of mood which so often came over her, when, instead of being the most lively company in the world, she was, all at once, silent and unresponsive, wrapped in thoughts whose strange gloom she could not explain. Then the cloud would pass, leaving Louisa as cheerful and as much in demand as before. The Alcott girls made a great addition to Mr. John Hosmer's district school. Louisa could run faster and jump higher than any other girl there and vault over fences with long-legged ease. She was always lamenting the fact that she was not born a boy.

The girls did not go to school a second year, but had lessons with their father and Mr. Henry Thoreau. Louisa seemed so much occupied with all the delights of a girl growing up, that it hardly seemed evident to anyone how deeply she had resolved to set her shoulder to the wheel of the family fortunes. When she reached sixteen she decided it was time to begin.

The barn, scene of her first dramatic triumph, was also the setting for her first venture in the greater enterprise of helping to take care of her dear family. She organized a little school there, probably at the suggestion of Mr. Emerson; for it was his children who made up the greater number of pupils. In spite of his great love for Bronson Alcott and his belief in his friend's ideas, Emerson chose Louisa, rather than her father, to teach his own children. Bronson had really great views upon education; but it fell to Louisa to translate those views into something which the young persons about her could truly absorb and understand.

What she had learned from her father made her a good teacher; but it could not make her love the task of instruction. Besides knowledge, she brought to the task energy and an enthusiasm for succeeding, along with that boundless friendliness which is the heart of a real teacher's success. The little girls got much from her; she in turn got much from them. There is no better way to learn how to understand the minds of children than to teach them. Louisa gave generously and taught well; but she could not learn to like her work. She was too restless and impetuous; she was too prone to find the long hours of sitting still as trying as did even the smallest of her pupils.

Determination, however, can take the place of patience, if earnestly applied. As Louisa sat at her desk, presiding over the small flock, her own thoughts, still busy with romance, flitted far above their labors, just as the steel-blue swallows were flitting high above amongst the rafters or skimming out through the open door into the sunshine. Little Ellen Emerson loved Louisa and was often at Hillside, in just the same way that Louisa ran in and out of the big white Emerson house. For her, Louisa began to write some stories, very different from those of her usual melodramatic style. They were about flowers and birds and fields, little fables which were the natural flowering in her own mind of what she had learned while teaching the school. After reading them to Ellen she tossed them aside amongst the plays and the tales of counts and nobles, which she so loved to compose. As yet few eyes beside her own had seen any of the scribbled manuscripts.

It may be guessed that the proceeds from this scholastic undertaking were not very great and were of far less value than the experience which came out of the summer's work. In the autumn certain questions became acute in the Alcott family. They had a roof over their heads, it was true. But with so little income it was impossible for Abba Alcott to see that the six members of the household were properly clothed and fed. Bronson Alcott must not be misjudged. He was untiringly industrious, and anxious above everything in the world to do what he could for his family. Yet it was impossible for him to find employment of any sort which would support them. He could not by the labor of his hands do enough work to supply all their wants. He knew much of farming but it had been proven at Fruitlands that his ideals and theories interfered with success even in that form of occupation. For commercial work he had no talent at all and could not be of any practical use in a counting house or in any pursuit of buying and selling. He was beloved by all who knew him and looked up to with admiration by everyone who understood what he had to offer. He gave lectures on Transcendental philosophy and on many others of the deep subjects being studied in that day. He was an excellent speaker, an exceedingly indifferent writer, a profound thinker, and a devoted friend. As a practical support for his family he was always striving, but in the eyes of the world never successful. He was to come into his own at last but it was not now.

As they had done at Fruitlands, the family held council over ways and means, an unhappy depressed council, for it was evident that the pleasant life they were leading at Hillside must come to an end. Mrs. Alcott had been offered employment in Boston, as an official visitor to the poor, and a brother had offered the family his house in which to live. It seemed that the necessities of food and raiment came before the affection they all had for friendly, happy Concord and the nearness of their guide, philosopher, and friend. The decision was made; they moved to town and once more entered upon a new era.

Louisa's experience with teaching gave her enough confidence to start bravely with the same sort of work in Boston. For two years she taught here and there, helped her mother, took care of small children as a nursery governess, sewed, did anything to which she could turn her hand. The family fortunes did not prosper very greatly, so that there were often difficult times in those various dwellings in which they lived, one after another. There was never depression or discouragement, however, for something ridiculous was always to be seen in every misadventure, something to call forth mirth and become the basis for a treasured family joke. Every evening they would gather about the lamp on the table and each one tell of the occurrences of the day, always making a good story of it, to the great entertainment of the rest. Anna was teaching, Louisa was doing a dozen things, May was going to school. When the record of their doings was complete, Mrs. Alcott would read to them or tell them ever-new tales of her own childhood and girlhood. One of her audience, at least, never forgot any of those stories.

One day there came to the house a gentleman in clerical garb who wished to consult Mrs. Alcott about finding a companion for his invalid sister. He wanted some "ladylike young woman, who would read to her, perform a few light household duties, and be treated exactly like a member of the family." People often came to Abba Alcott on such errands; for part of her work was the keeping of an intelligence office to find places for the needy women in whom she was interested. There was nothing unusual in the errand of this stranger, except that the position he described seemed so marvelously easy and pleasant. Whoever came to them, so it seemed, would have all the comforts and the considerations of a very good home.

Louisa overheard him and was fired with enthusiasm. She would love to take the place herself. She was eighteen; she had done no work so far except amongst friends and acquaintances;

but this was too great an opportunity to miss. She pictured easily the interesting, suffering sister, the great comfortable house, the figure of herself, flitting about, distributing comfort and cheerfulness and being loved and appreciated in return. When her mother asked her if she had any person to suggest she responded instantly, "Only myself."

After the man was gone, Abba Alcott reasoned with her daughter a little, since it was a most impulsive decision. But with Louisa, all conclusions came rapidly, and to this rosy plan she clung with persistence. The man had been asked about wages, but his reply had been slightly vague. There would be no occasion to use such a vulgar term as wages, he asserted; the young companion was to be so much a part of the family that wages was not the word. Certainly she would be well compensated, but payment would be offered under some more suitable name. Louisa's sisters laughed at her and her mother still offered protest; but the girl was firm. They were in such need that it was not wise to let any proper opening escape her. She did not stop to think that she was taking up employment with total strangers, without any definite agreement as to the matter of salary, and without real understanding of what her duties were to be. On the appointed day she betook herself to the address which had been given her, and was duly introduced to Miss Eliza, the ailing sister, who was a "martyr to neuralgia." Louisa agreed to a trial on both sides for a month.

What a wretched awakening followed! In that cold, dismal house, a feeble old father dozed all day; the invalid sister sat about, helpless and unhappy; a very ancient serving woman trudged back and forth in the kitchen, unable to compass more than the meager cooking which the household afforded. Reading aloud? Such a thing was never thought of. Light duties? They consisted of bringing in coal from the shed and water from the well, carrying the heavy burdens up long, steep stairs, sifting ashes, shoveling snow from the walks, cleaning and scrubbing when nothing else was insistently necessary. Inwardly Louisa raged, stormed to herself, but admitted with sturdy honesty that she had brought the whole of the misery upon her own head.

She had promised to stay a month and stay she did, carrying ashes, splitting wood, making fires, and waiting upon the plaintive invalid. In all this time nothing was said about paying her. The brother who had employed her treated her with lofty disdain and one day took her to task for not performing the whole of her duties. He observed coldly that she had not cleaned his boots and directed that she should do so.

No, she would not. She made no attempt to gild the refusal; she was sorry for Miss Eliza and the doddering old father, but she had small respect for the man whose misrepresentations had brought her to this pass. He attempted to show injured dignity and to insist; but he got nowhere. Louisa decidedly would not black his boots.

Late that evening she heard a small noise in the dim corridor and, peeping out of her door, caught sight of the dignified gentleman sorrowfully collecting brushes and rags and boots and attacking the hated task himself. Louisa enjoyed the prospect for a long time, shivering in the cold, delighted to have found one thing at last in this wretched house over which she could laugh, even though all alone. When the unhappy month was nearly over, she announced in no uncertain terms that she would not stay longer. Poor Miss Eliza wept so pitifully that Louisa, too impulsive again, agreed to remain until someone else could be found. Two others came in turn, looked about them briefly, called Louisa a fool, and went away.

Three weeks passed while she still toiled on. When the third victim arrived, she gave her no time to consider. Her small effects were packed and the moment the substitute came in at the door, Louisa betook herself to the sitting room and bade the household farewell. The gentleman who had hired her had disappeared from sight. The old father spoke shakily of his sorrow over her going and the unfortunate Miss Eliza wept anew. She put a small pocketbook into Louisa's hand, the payment for her seven weeks of hard labor. As Louisa went downstairs, the old servant emerged from the kitchen to look strangely at the little purse in the girl's red, chapped hand and to make the ominous remark:

"Don't blame us for anything; some folks is liberal and some ain't."

"Don't blame us!" Queer devotion which identified itself with this ungenerous family and made the toiling old woman the one memorable and admirable figure in that sordid place. As she walked away from the house Louisa was exultant over one thing. Her own family needed money sorely and she had earned it for them! Stopping in the chilly, wind-swept street, she opened the pocket book. Within was four dollars, the sum total of her wages! Four dollars for seven weeks of cruelly unhappy toil! Louisa was not prone to be bitter, but bitter anger swept through her then; she had hoped so much, had given so much, and this was what they thought was the appropriate return. It was not love of money, not even the need of it, which made that moment so hard. It was the disillusionment, the knowledge that anyone could treat her so, could take her trusting, eager service and dismiss her with such a pitiful reward as this.

She laughed over most of her impetuous mistakes, but there is no record that either she or her sisters ever made sport of this sorry experience. When she showed the money at home, it was characteristic of the Alcotts that the immediate step taken was to return it. Bronson, moved to rare anger, wanted to lay violent hands upon the man in the garb of a minister who had come to his house and made such misstatements to warmhearted, credulous Louisa. In the effort to calm him, the rest of the family forgot a little of their righteous wrath. Louisa scarcely ever mentioned that incident in her life in all the years following. Truly it attacked her very faith in the goodness of mankind. It was an experience of some value but of miserable memory.

Thus material matters continued to go badly with the Alcotts. Plainness of living they did not mind. Had they not learned that every sort of plainness can accompany the real treasure of spiritual life? But even amid their cheerfulness and good spirits there were moments of such hardship that the present seemed bad and the future desperately insecure. One plan was always at the back of Louisa's mind. She had very beautiful and very long, dark hair, "not just the fashionable color," as we are told, but of wonderful luxuriance. An exuberance of hair was as fashionable then as it is unfashionable today; chignons, waterfalls, and cascades of curls were a necessity, whether they flourished naturally or not. Louisa's hair, which almost touched the ground when let out of its net, was the envy of all her feminine friends. It was, in her mind, her reserve capital. When affairs were at a desperate pass with the Alcott fortunes, she went one day to a barber, let down the cloud of dark hair and asked him what he would give for it.

The sum he named seemed vast wealth to her, but she could not make up her mind to the sacrifice at once. Unless matters mended within seven days, she told herself sternly, her hair should go. It was like laying her neck upon the block, for cropped heads looked ugly then, and Louisa's, with her tall figure, would seem more awkward than another's. The week passed and Providence, in the guise of a generous friend, saved Louisa's hair. Substantial help came suddenly from a hand accustomed to offering assistance. There is reason to believe that it was Mr. Emerson's.

In the summer of that same year the family all fell ill with smallpox, caught from some destitute emigrants who had come begging to the gate, and whom Mrs. Alcott had brought into the garden and fed. Abba Alcott and Bronson were very ill; the girls only slightly so. Anna and Louisa nursed their parents through those desperate days with no help from outside. Not a neighbor came near them, nor a doctor. An unquenchable family, they survived the ordeal without despair or bitterness and girded themselves to face the world again.

Life in a city was not really the proper one for these four growing girls, especially a restricted, grubbing life such as they were forced to lead. After the smallpox experience the Alcotts left their uncle's house and took a place in High Street. Abba went to her work every day, May to school, Bronson to his lectures, Anna and Louisa taught, while Elizabeth, now seventeen, did the housekeeping. "Our angel in a cellar kitchen," Louisa speaks of her thus, with resentment and rebellion. They moved finally to Pinckney Street, where Mrs. Alcott kept boarders so that she might be at home with her children. Bronson had gone on a journey into the West to lecture. Boarders do not pay much at best and are apt to play upon the feelings of a kindhearted landlady. Finances were still very low and great hopes were built upon what was to come out of the lecturing. It is a famous incident, that night in a cold February, when Bronson returned home late, chilled and tired from his long travel. Everyone rushed down to hug and embrace him, to ply him with comforts, and to rejoice over his return. After the first flurry was over there was, suddenly, a little silence, of waiting, of wondering. It was enterprising May who broke it.

"Well, did they pay you?"

Very slowly, Bronson drew out his pocketbook and displayed its contents. He had come home from far journeys before, after those excursions into Virginia, having gathered the riches of learning new things on the way and having left the riches of his glowing thoughts wherever he passed. Fortunes had always been varying; he had returned from the South sometimes prosperous, sometimes bankrupt. It mattered little to him then; it mattered little now, as he drew forth the fruit of his enterprise—a single dollar.

"Another year, I shall do better," he observed cheerfully.

There was a minute of choking silence.

"I call that doing *very well*," said Abba Alcott suddenly, as she threw her arms about his neck.

Louisa, watching in the lamplight, saw all at once what real love can do, what heights it can reach. She knew very clearly how her mother had hoped, what were the things she might have said; she knew what courage was behind those words of approval and affection.

A great event had occurred during this period and had been brought about through Bronson's means. He found one of Louisa's little flower fables written for Ellen Emerson in Concord; he showed it to a publishing friend and it had been approved, actually accepted, bought, and printed! A very small incident, apparently, scarcely making a ripple on the surface of literary affairs. In spite of her inward excitement, Louisa called it a little matter also and cheerily pronounced the story "great rubbish." The tales of wild adventure were still far more to her taste. She was writing them busily whenever her varied wage earning gave her a moment to attend to them. Her brain was teeming with plots and excitements every hour as she went about sewing and teaching and watching over children. She said very little to anyone of all that was going on within herself.

The little story was liked and the rest of the stories written for Ellen Emerson were gathered together and published in a small book, *Flower Fables*. Louisa could actually be spoken of as an author, although she made great game of herself in light of such a role.

The following summer she was invited by good Cousin Lizzie Wells to spend some time in Walpole, New Hampshire. It was pleasant to be in the green hills again, to take long walks through the fields and feel the fresh wind blowing about her. She wrote more flower stories here and began to think more seriously of what she might be able to do with her pen, of what she could accomplish for her family. Her mother decided finally that the life in the city was assuredly not the thing for her children, where they had barely enough kept their heads above water in spite of their cheerful struggle and their continual insistence that all was well. She moved to Walpole with the rest, and settled down to spend the winter. It was then that Louisa came to a great resolve.

She had never been any distance from her mother before, had never taken any momentous step without the support of her family behind her. But she found that she could earn nothing in Walpole and that as the weeks passed she was too restless even to write. She would set out alone, she concluded, and, if she could do no more, could earn her own living and be less of a care to her family. It was not an easy decision for a shy, untrained girl to make, in a time when work for young women, especially young women of the class called ladies, was extraordinarily difficult to find.

It was November; it was chilly and raining that day she set her face alone to the great world. She had a very little money, a small trunk, a package of manuscripts, and an enormous fund of hope and determination. The rumbling stage carried her out of sight of the little house amongst the New Hampshire hills. It bore her down the roads lined with leafless maples, between the gray stone walls and the tangles of frost-bitten blackberry bushes. Courage, terror, dismay, and relentless determination were all in her heart as she heard the hollow rumble of the wheels on the covered wooden bridge and knew that she was actually launched upon the first enterprise of seeking her fortunes single-handed.

# CHAPTER FIVE

### ᘒ᠍᠍᠍ ᘒ᠍᠍᠍ ᘒ᠍᠍᠍

## "The Girl I Left Behind Me"

NO ONE WILL EVER KNOW HOW HARD FOR Louisa were those first years of making her way alone. Excessive shyness is not the best equipment for facing a strange and unreceptive world already overcrowded with those struggling for a living. Louisa was not only shy, but she was very sensitive, as all creative persons must be. To offset such handicaps she had only courage, unquenchable courage, which could usually laugh at hurt feelings and discomfitures and always rose from a fall to try again.

Her cousins, the Sewalls, gave her a place to stay that winter, while she worked at teaching, sewing, at anything to which she could turn her industrious hands. She wrote and wrote and wrote. The stories were strange, melodramatic, lurid compositions, still full of matter of which she really knew nothing. They were vigorously written, however, and began to be sold for small sums here and there. Bronson Alcott had taken one of them to a friend of his who was then editor of a famous magazine.

"Tell Louisa to stick to her teaching," the gentleman said kindly. "She is never going to be a writer."

Was Louisa crushed when she heard of his verdict? "I will *not* stick to my teaching; I *will* be a writer," she declared. "And I will write for his magazine too."

She did, but not during this difficult period.

A friend of her mother's had three young daughters, two of whom Louisa had taught while the Alcotts still lived in Boston. The youngest was an invalid and could not go to school. Louisa taught her for part of every day and spent the rest of the time in sewing and writing. People were not particularly kind to anyone in Louisa's struggling position. Teaching was really considered to be the only fairly respectable pursuit for young ladies, and even that was looked down upon by those who thought at that time that leisure was more dignified than work. Louisa had no such false ideas; she was, moreover, spurred by an indomitable purpose. She was not only going to support herself but she was later going to uphold the family fortunes. At first it was all that she possibly could do to stand upon her own feet.

She was worn out with discouragement and was presently made more unhappy by bad news from the little house in the New Hampshire hills. Mrs. Alcott had interested herself in a very poor family there, where some children were ill from living in an unsanitary house. The owner, a deacon of the church, refused to have it put in order until spirited Abba Alcott said that she would bring suit against him. When he gave in it was too late; the children in the family were sick with scarlet fever. The contagion was carried to the Alcott house and May and Elizabeth both were taken ill. Elizabeth was in great danger for some time, so that Louisa was summoned from Boston. Quiet little Elizabeth, unhappy over a small love affair which had not gone properly, very ill besides, was near to death but finally won her way back to some semblance of the health she had known before. It was not until autumn that Louisa set forth again, this time with a desperately heavy heart. Elizabeth did not get back any real strength and they were all seriously anxious about her. The family in Walpole was slowly coming to the decision to return to Concord where Betty could be nearer to medical advice and where Bronson could be far happier in the neighborhood of his dear friend Emerson.

Louisa declared that she could try Boston again, being "wiser for her failures," as she said. She wrote in her journal:

"I don't often pray in words, but when I set out that day, with all my goods in a little old trunk, my own (very small) earnings in my pocket, and much hope and resolution in my soul, my heart was very full, and I said to the Lord, 'Help us all and keep us for one another,' as I never said it before, while I looked back at the dear faces watching me, so full of love and hope and faith."

It is pathetic to think what faith they all had in her — poor, toiling Louisa. It must have been hard indeed to go away with that threatening shadow already upon the house.

She returned to Boston in the hope that she could once more teach the little invalid Alice, but the first news which met her was that she would not be needed. That was not cheering but she did not lose heart. At the boarding house of Mrs. Reed she arranged to have a little attic room in return for which she was to sew a certain number of hours every day. But she must find something further to do; for merely a roof over her head was not enough. Search for employment was unusually disheartening, but various things happened to cheer her. Cousin Lizzie Wells gave her tickets to a course of lectures, great riches to Louisa, to whom such opportunities were not often open. The practical cousin appended to the gift the present of a coat in which to go to the lectures, an exceedingly thoughtful addition. Another cousin procured for Louisa a pass to go to the theater, so that she revelled in high dramatic moments. She was sent for at last to go to Beacon Street, to teach little Alice, after all; and with her sewing and the sale of stories she began to feel safely independent. No matter how busy she was she managed to find time to teach in a little mission Sunday school, what we would now call a settlement. It was one of the Alcott beliefs that no matter how poor a person is he or she always had something which could be given away.

Louisa was very homesick. From the beginning of the time that she knew how to write she had kept a journal, at first full of brief entries put down in a large misshapen hand, interspersed with little notes by her mother. It was Abba Alcott's habit to look into the diaries which were always open to her and to write brief letters to her children amongst the pages of uncertain writing. "I have observed all day your patience with baby, your obedience to me, your kindness to all." After one of Louisa's tempests of furious temper which broke out from time to time when she was small was this comment, "I was grieved at your selfish behaviour this morning but also greatly pleased to find you bore so meekly Father's reproof of it. I know that you will have a happy day after the storm; keep quiet, read, walk, but do not talk much till all is peace again." The girl's outbursts were of a somewhat different style now, although more than once she resented hotly the fact that things were so easy for many whom she saw about her and so hard for her beloved family, that care should so weigh down her courageous mother. After the storm, however, always came determination; things should be better, they would be made so by Louisa. She missed her mother's wise presence and the cheery notes; but she struggled forward.

Cousin Lizzie Wells had given her a dress, "my first, new silk dress," as Louisa recorded it.

"I felt as if all the Hancocks and the Quincys beheld me as I went to two parties in it on New Years's Eve," her journal declared. Possibly she was conscious that, on certain occasions, the Quincys and the Hancocks would not have quite approved of all the casual doings and the informal costumes of the Alcott connection.

One happiness was always open to her. On Sunday evenings she would go to the house of some dear friends of her father's and of her own, Mr. and Mrs. Theodore Parker. Next to the Emersons, perhaps even equal to them, were these friends, in their influence on Louisa's life. Theodore Parker had been brought up on a farm outside Lexington, only a few miles from Concord, and loved all that rock-dotted, pine-clad, farming country as she did, and, as she knew, dreamed of it in the crowded narrow streets of Boston.

His struggle for an education had been something like her father's, although he had got his learning by great effort from Harvard. He became finally a minister and at this time in Boston was a commanding figure in the religious life and in the political thought of the time.

Calm Boston was beginning to seethe with excitement, as it had not done since the storm of the Revolution was gathering, since the great moment of the Boston Tea Party.

The feeling against slavery, long held in check, was now rolling up into a tremendous wave which was to break, crashing into the vast catastrophe of war. Louisa could remember that her father's friend, William Lloyd Garrison, was dragged through the streets by a mob "made up of gentlemen of substance and property" who threatened to hang him for being an Abolitionist.

Now a mob, wrought to a high pitch by a very different feeling, rescued the fugitive slave, Shadrach, and carried him away to liberty. Again when the runaway Negro, Burns, was lodged in the city jail, preparatory to returning him to his master as was now the strict law, once more a mob attempted to assault the prison for the purpose of setting him free. He was too well guarded, however, and there was not sufficient plan amongst the rescuers to accomplish their ends. A deputy marshal was killed; revolvers drove back the crowd, the last to retreat being none other than Bronson Alcott.

Theodore Parker, staid and eminent minister, "the most crowd-drawing preacher in Boston," as Lowell described him, concealed a runaway slave woman in his house. He sat, with a drawn pistol on the table beside him, writing his sermon for the next Sunday, ready, in case of any immediate interruption by the officers of the law, to defend the poor fugitive to the point of bloodshed.

A picturesque adventure of his was that concerning Ellen Craft and her husband, William. The two Negroes had fled from the South and were hidden in different places in and about Boston for a number of months. Whispers of their whereabouts having come to the ears of the authorities, there was finally such danger of their being captured and taken back that arrangements were made by their anti-slavery friends to smuggle them to England.

The night before they were to be put on board ship, they sent for Theodore Parker. They had something to explain to him, a great service to ask. They were husband and wife, but not by any formal marriage. The institution of slavery did not take any special account of marriage; if a man were sold away from his wife, both of them under new masters were supposed to take new mates. But these two, whom nothing could part, wanted now to be really married as free people were. They begged that Parker perform the service over them before they sailed.

In the dark little boarding house, their last refuge before putting to sea, he went through the marriage ceremony. Armed men guarded the door, lest there be interruption. Into the body of the prayers and vows Parker introduced the stern admonition that the husband must "defend his wife's liberty against all comers." As the service closed, the minister took up two gifts and handed them to the bridegroom: a Bible, "for the defense of your soul," he said, and a great bowie knife, "for the defense of your body."

There is no wonder that Louisa loved and admired such a man. Comfortable, sympathetic Mrs. Parker, befriending people in unending numbers, was interested in Louisa, came to see her in her sky parlor, and was always delighted to welcome her to their house where the truly great people of the time came together. Mr. Parker, a sturdy figure, not very tall, a man with direct, blue-gray eyes and a straight, determined mouth, went here and there amongst his guests.

110

He had not much time for the tall, bashful girl in the corner, but he had always the right word. "Well, child, how goes it? Pretty well? That's brave," and he would go on to speak to someone else. He would bid her good-night — "God bless you, Louisa, come again — " and she would go home brave with the pure contagion of a dauntless spirit.

"He is like a great fire," she said of him in her journal, "where all can come and be warmed and comforted."

When June came she went back to Walpole, increasingly troubled about Elizabeth. When she saw her, after her weeks of absence, she realized the desperate possibility which was before them all. The move to Concord, long weighed, was now decided upon. After much thought it was agreed that it would be better to buy a house and revive if it were still possible something of the easy happiness of those earlier days at Hillside. That house was no longer available; it belonged now to a friend of the Alcotts', a shy man grown to be famous and hating his prominence—Nathaniel Hawthorne. A place a little nearer the town was possible to procure, however, a piece of ground lying below the same ridge of pine- and birch-grown hill, fronting also on the Lexington road. There was a house upon the land, so old and dilapidated a building that the former owner "threw it in with the bargain," not counting it as possible that anything could be done with it but to tear it down. He did not know the resourceful Allcotts.

Mrs. Alcott took Elizabeth to Boston while Louisa and Anna attended to the affairs of moving. They packed again — how many times was it now? They had not the heart to try to remember. So much had to be done to the old house in which they meant to live that they were obliged to take other quarters for the immediate present, part of a double house near the Concord Town Hall. A room was made comfortable for Lizzie and all the old-time neighbors came pouring in to welcome the Alcotts back to Concord. Bronson, Louisa, Anna, and May fell to work to see what could be done with the newly acquired dwelling. There were fruit trees about it, so that it was christened officially Orchard House. Louisa, however, had a different name for it. In their family there was a certain New England pudding made of apples, a homely dish, much loved by them all but of no great elegance. She named the house after it — Apple Slump.

The poor, dejected old dwelling, which must somehow be a home to them, seemed to take kindly to the name. It began to come to life quite suddenly under their hands. Bronson worked hard upon the grounds for he had a gift

112

with gardens and made this one prosper. The untended fruit trees were cared for, the growth cleared away from about the hundred-year-old elm which stood near the gate and which had seen the minutemen go by. Anna and Louisa scrubbed and polished, contrived closets and cupboards, made the most of the old beams and rafters, and turned dusty corners into alcoves for books. All three of the girls painted and papered, while May made decorative panels for the walls. Their friend, William Ellery Channing, composed a motto for the low-ceiled room at the left of the doorway which was to be Bronson's study. May painted the words over the chimneypiece:

"The hills are reared, the valleys scooped in
    vain,
    If Learning's altars vanish from the plain."

They worked all through the winter, since without money they could make no great speed.

For Elizabeth's sake they strove to seem to be happy and presently through the very effort accomplished something of the reality. Mr. Frank B. Sanborn, another dear and distinguished friend, had a school for boys not far away. The girls threw themselves into the dramatics there and organized, coached, and staged many a thrilling or comic play. Elizabeth loved to see the preparations, to watch the costumes take shape, and to hear of the success with which these efforts were received. It was like the days of Roderigo's boots come back again.

The Miss Elizabeth Peabody, dear friend of them all, who had been Mr. Alcott's assistant at the Temple School, and for whom Elizabeth Alcott was named, had a sister who had also helped there. This sister had married Nathaniel Hawthorne, and her children, some years younger than the Alcotts, lived near and were constant companions of the four girls. Julian Hawthorne, who was attending the Sanborn School, went past the house every day and always stopped for talk and laughter. He was somewhat younger than May, the youngest Alcott; but it was one of Louisa's family jokes that he had developed a tender passion for this younger sister. Louisa used to hold forth on the hopelessness of poor Julian's attachment, since a mythical "cousin from England," a vague person of highest rank and fortune, was to arrive some day and carry May away to pursue life in the exalted ranks of the titled great.

One evening, just at dusk, Julian was walking down the road past the house, when a strange and horrifying sight met him. May was standing at the gate, and beside her was a tall stranger, carrying a foppish cane, dressed with a slight eccentricity which must be foreign, possessed of bold dark eyes and a small black mustache. The astounding thing was that his arm was about May's waist, evidently without her protest or objection.

Julian approached, his eyes fairly starting from his head, and was introduced to "our cousin." The foreigner stepped forward, bowed, and acknowledged the introduction with an insolent patronage of manner which the boy could not endure.

"Well, well, so this is our young friend Julian; quite a well-grown boy!"

Intolerable talk to a lad who had cast something in the nature of adoring eyes at May! Julian stepped up to the stranger and was received by a flourish of the cane in his face, twirled with apparent carelessness by the English youth, but nonetheless uncomfortably and threateningly near. The American boy clenched his fists, and suddenly May, apparently overcome, turned and took flight toward the house. The Englishman took one more provocative step forward, then amazingly snatched off the black mustache and threw it over Julian's head, following it with the black felt hat which had created such a rakish foreign impression. The removal of the hat brought down a flood of dark hair. Julian Hawthorne said of the scene, long afterward:

"Then Louisa turned and pursued May up the path, whooping like a Comanche, but with a feminine consciousness, I fancied, of the pantaloons."

It was, perhaps, their last hilarious occasion. As the autumn and winter drew on, Elizabeth became steadily worse. By January, all knew that nothing further was to be done; even she herself knew it and faced the end with that inflexible, heroic bravery that so often resides in quiet people. She loved to have Louisa near her. "It makes me feel strong," so she said. Anna took charge of the house, while Louisa and her mother gave themselves up to nursing.

It was March when Elizabeth went away. Louisa saw her go with that strange, numb calmness that attends an agonizing grief when it cannot be averted. Elizabeth was glad to be at rest; no one could begrudge her the freedom from suffering which she had finally won, when "on the same breast where she had drawn her first breath, she quietly drew her last." An inconspicuous, beautiful, unselfish life, coming to an imperceptible close. In the next year, Theodore Parker was to die, and Louisa was to go to the vast memorial service in Music Hall, where floods of sunshine, great heaps of flowers, and the eloquence of the foremost men of his day were to bear witness to his greatness. And yet more hearts, thousands more, perhaps, have been wrung by the death of Elizabeth Alcott, unassuming, courageous little Beth, than by the passing of that famous man. Why? Not through Louisa's genius alone, but through the unsurpassed beauty of that life which it was Louisa's privilege to picture — when the time came.

Life goes on after sorrow, in spite of sorrow, as a defense against sorrow. Louisa had a burden of debt to carry now, a sordid addition to her weight of grief. The money which had bought the old house was a little, carefully guarded capital of Mrs. Alcott's, left her by her father. The great step of spending it had been decided on in the hope that it might save Elizabeth, or give her a happy comfortable place in which to spend her last days of life. It had accomplished neither. Louisa cherished an unreasoned enmity for the house forever after, knowing that the feeling was not just, but still unable to restrain it. They were committed to live there now, however, and must go forward with their preparations.

The Hawthornes, who had bought Hillside, were to be away, and offered the Alcotts the use of their place until the repairs on Orchard House should at last be finished. So the family moved into one wing, and Louisa lived again for a few months where they had been so happy in those first rich years. They were still here when another change came upon them, a thing against which Louisa stormed aloud, although she must surely have foreseen its coming.

There is always a memory of comradeship between people who have had in common certain outstanding adventures of life. At the time that the Fruitlands enterprise was going on, various other experiments in community living were being tried in other places. A number of people whom Bronson and Abba Alcott knew were concerned with Brook Farm, where lived a company of people who held their property in common, as did the community at Fruitlands. It was a larger undertaking than the Fruitlands experiment and lasted a little longer, and while it came to an end through disagreement of its members as all such experiments did, it was not concluded under the same cloud of tragedy as was Bronson Alcott's unhappy venture. Emerson was interested in both of them; Nathaniel Hawthorne was one of the Brook Farm members, as were also a family of Hosmers and a family of Pratts. Hawthorne and Emerson were the Alcotts' dear friends always; so were the Hosmers, who took the destitute family into their own house when the move was made from

Still River back to Concord. Without that connection it is probable that Bronson would not have let his girls go to their single term of school; for it was John Hosmer, of the same same family, who taught them that winter. There were also close bonds between the Alcotts and the Pratts who had taken a farm of their own after Brook Farm ended and had lived there ever since. At this time of sorrow Anna went to visit the Pratts in the country and came home to give the family news of great import. She walked into the parlor and launched the momentous tidings at once. She was engaged to the son of the house, John Bridge Pratt.

Once, in the Hillside days, a boy in the midst of a game at a party had kissed Anna. Louisa raged and stormed over such impertinence and always forever after spoke of the unfortunate youth with scorn. Kissing was not an approved custom among the Alcotts. She raged in much the same manner now. She wanted Anna to be happy. She liked John Pratt, but why, oh, why, should families have to separate? She lamented continually and bitterly although not in Anna's hearing.

Cousin Lizzie Wells came to the rescue while Louisa was in this distracted mood and carried her away for a visit in Boston. It was during that brief stay that Louisa put into execution a long-laid plan. She determined now to make a real, definite effort to go upon the stage. Money was earned so slowly by sewing and writing and the pursuit of it was so humdrum. If she could only have adventure and excitement and applause, and could reap the financial rewards that sounded so dazzling and golden, what could she not do then for her beloved ones! A friend of her father's, Doctor Winship, had given her an introduction to a certain manager, a Mr. Barry.

To this Mr. Barry she repaired and asked if he would give her a place for trial. Would he let her appear, she requested, just to see what she could do with comedy. The manager looked her over attentively, a tall girl, with a big mouth, brilliant eyes, and a mass of wavy chestnut hair. Her features were not beautiful but her expression was; for it lighted her face and made her not only striking, but lovely. No one who looked at her ever failed to see the strong character and earnest purpose which always burned behind those dark eyes.

Mr. Barry hesitated, knowing that a young person "of her connections" did not often offer herself for life on the stage. He demurred; but her enthusiasm overbore him and he found himself promising her a place. Would she care to try the Widow Pottle, a character part and a very small one? She would indeed. It was better, they both agreed, that no one should know who she was until after the trial had been made. She went out from the interview in a mood of high exaltation. Mr. Barry may have thought that the whole thing was something of a joke, the cheerful prank of a spirited young lady. To her, it was a matter of tremendous importance. Already, as she walked home, she was seeing visions of herself in the life of an actress. Memories of the first pleasant flush of success came back to her, the recollection of the drama in the old barn, when she had trod the boards in Roderigo's boots.

No one with such soaring hopes as Louisa had could fail to be disappointed, not once, but many times in life. Long after, she once said of herself that disappointment must be good for her, she got so much of it. She learned to meet it bravely, although often she felt at first only a hot wave of revolt. Disappointment came now; for Mr. Barry was hurt in an accident and the play containing the Widow Pottle had to be given up. Louisa stormed again; for it seemed as though misfortune were singling her out, of special purpose. After a day of lamentation she faced the issue bravely. She admitted to herself that she had craved the unusualness and the exciting stimulus of such a life, rather than that she had felt any great call to it. She steadied her spirits and went home to Concord to help the others settle at last in the Orchard House, to enjoy the look of peace on her mother's face, as she went about in a dwelling which at last seemed tolerably permanent.

Louisa wrote busily all summer, always with the interesting spur of some special thing she wanted to get for the new household, a carpet, a ream of paper for her father, or dresses for various members of the family. Between tales, she got out her "best silk dress" and made it over, the same one which Cousin Lizzie Wells had given her years before. It was a dark summer for her, with one parting behind her and another before her, and a sense of rebellion still that such things should separate the people she loved. In the autumn she went once more to Boston to see what work she could find to do.

At no time in her life had she ever fallen so low in spirits as now. She was discontented with her old drudging ways of making a living; she was lonely, sad, and unbelievably disheartened. She was full of life always; but now she wished suddenly and deeply that she could die. She did not want to go on living in a world where everything was so hard. She trudged here and there looking for employment and did not find it. That seemed almost the last detail of discouraging circumstance. But unquenchable Louisa was not utterly submerged, even now.

"There is work for me to do and I will find it," she told herself fiercely and in that very challenge overthrew something of her discouragement.

It was on her dreariest and most disheartened Sunday that she went to hear Theodore Parker preach. By one of those rare coincidences which are more than chance, his sermon that day was, so it seemed, for her alone. "Laborious Young Women" was the subject; for he had deemed it time to say some word to those misunderstood toiling girls for whom there were so few opportunities and so little encouragement. He poured out for them that blessing of knowledge concerning which he was so sure, that absolute certainty of where they were to look for sustaining help when the way seemed impossible to pursue further.

For Louisa that Sunday service was a landmark in her life. It was like that morning when she was a little girl and saw the sun coming up over the Concord meadows and the silent river, when she knew suddenly all the beauty and goodness of God. She felt that she understood ever after what God was. Today, sitting in the crowded church, she went forward to a new feeling; she understood what God wanted her to do. She had never lost heart so completely before; she was never to lose it again in just that way. There was one, at least, in Theodore Parker's

123

congregation that day who carried away courage and faith to such a degree that if he had reached no other heart his preaching would have been gloriously repaid. Louisa was probably only one of hundreds who heard and were comforted. She was one who not only pondered upon his counsel but set out immediately with her usual energy to put it into effect.

She went to Mrs. Parker and asked if she knew of something — anything — which an energetic girl could do to help her family. There was nothing immediately available, but good, ever-helpful Mrs. Parker would see. As she walked home Louisa met the mother of her little invalid pupil, Alice. The child had been considered well enough at last to go to school and had not needed Louisa's instruction. Alice was not happy at school, her mother said now; perhaps they would have Louisa to teach her, after all. She would send word later. Louisa went home and waited but no word came. In the meantime a place was offered her through Mrs. Parker. Would she go to the Girls' Reform School at Lancaster to sew ten hours a day on uniforms and on mending sheets and towels? Louisa listened to the suggestion with a surge of repulsion. To work in a prison, to sew from morning until night, with no time for anything else! But she must find something; and this was all that was available.

"If Alice's mother does not take me I will go," she determined. Another day passed. She packed her belongings, made her preparations, hating the prospect with all the force of her spirit, but bound that she would carry out her resolution to take what work she could do. The last evening, just as she was about to leave, came a knock on the door and a message. Alice and her mother wanted her again; a salary was offered which would make it possible for her to live in Boston, to occupy her little sky parlor once more, and to write. She sent word in a great splendid wave of relief, that she would stay. There were other people to take the Girls' Reform School work, people who were not young and sensitive and discouraged. They were not in the depths of a depression which needed above all things some brighter atmosphere than that prevailing in a women's prison in the 1850's. Such were not cheerful or wholesome places for persons of Louisa's temperament. Mrs. Parker had grieved over it but had felt that it was better than nothing. When she told her husband how Louisa had stood to her determination to the very last minute, Theodore Parker uttered a solemn prophecy:

"Louisa," he said, "is going to succeed."

He did not live to see his words fulfilled; for he was already in the grip of that illness which was to end his life a few months later. But he had his great share in her success, nonetheless.

In the spring Louisa went home to Anna's wedding. A very simple ceremony it was, but with such dear friends to attend it, and with such deep happiness everywhere, that it seemed to stand apart from other weddings. Abba Alcott's brother, Samuel Joseph May, performed the marriage. He had married Abba and Bronson, on the same day and month, thirty-one years earlier. The wedding at Orchard House ended with a dance on the grass outside under the great elm. Louisa felt very old and bereft and lonely; but romance was not all gone. She put down in her diary that night,

"Mr. Emerson kissed Anna; and I thought that honor would make even matrimony endurable."

She may not have remained in that mood long, however; for a little later she wrote after going to see Anna in her new house and observing her sister's happiness in her new life —

"Very sweet and pretty; but I would rather be a free spinster and paddle my own canoe."

It was while she was still at home that the news reached her of the death of Theodore Parker. "I am glad to have known so good a man," she wrote of him. Behind that simple statement is all her gratitude for the cheerful welcomes when she was lonely and homesick, for counsel and encouragement in the midst of a great man's busy days, for the fortitude which he put into her heart, to remain there forever.

May had gone to teach in Syracuse where their uncle, Samuel Joseph May, lived. Now that Anna was away, Louisa remained at home to help with the household and to earn what she could by her writing. She was restless and unstrung; for not only had unsettling changes come about in her own family but the shadow of an enormous change was reaching over the whole country. No one could doubt now that there was going to be war. And as Louisa often said darkly to herself, "I'm a fighting May." This was the summer of 1860, and the tempest though near had not yet broken.

Louisa's profession was beginning to prosper a little, although what she earned by her romantic tales was hardly more than a pittance. She realized that she was not doing her best even though she had achieved now her great desire; she was writing stories for that famous magazine whose editor had told her to "stick to her teaching." She began on a novel and, growing more and more absorbed in it, she wrote day and night, burning with enthusiasm, afraid that the idea might escape her before it could be set safely on paper. The book was called *Moods*, her first long story. By winter she had written herself out on it and put it aside for another novel which she called *Success*. In it appeared Theodore Parker under the name of Mr. Powers. It was the first time that she had tried putting a definite person into any of her tales.

Bronson Alcott had been going nearly every summer to make a lecture tour of the West, holding Conversations, as he always called them. He was doing better and better with them, as after the first endeavor he had so cheerfully prophesied that he would. Now another pleasant thing was to come which gladdened the hearts of all who had loved him so truly and who had winced under the misunderstanding which so far was all that the world had offered him. Through the offices of Mr. Emerson he was made superintendent of schools in Concord and had a chance finally to see a growing generation of children get the benefit of what he knew to be the proper way of teaching. He had always known so well that the dreariness and the long hours should be ended, that the dark rooms and the harsh pressure on struggling minds should be done away with. He had to wait very patiently until the world should begin to know it too. We realize it a hundred times better now, seventy years later; and we have most of us forgotten that Bronson Alcott knew all these things the very first of us all.

He was loved in the schools and was applauded and approved, after such long waiting to be understood. When the spring term came to an end there was a school festival with singing and marching, with little girls in white dresses and little boys in clean ruffled shirts. There had never been such a thing before. At the very end, a tall, good-looking boy came forward with a package, "from the children of Concord, as a token of our love and respect." Bronson opened the paper—it was a beautifully bound book. Can anyone guess what book? It was *Pilgrim's Progress.* That beautiful copy which belonged to the Temple School was gone forever, but here was another in its place, a treasure which could push aside at last a very bitter memory. Bronson Alcott blushed and stammered and the children cheered until the big school building rocked again.

It was close on the heels of that happy episode that there came another event, the overpowering news of the firing on Fort Sumter, the opening gun of the Civil War. People heard those tidings and were stunned, as though the roar of the cannon was in their very ears. War seems a perfectly impossible thing, even when it can be seen coming nearer and nearer. It is still impossible to believe in when it has actually arrived. But it is so tremendous a fact that everyone must believe in the end for everyone must bear his share.

During the first year Louisa did what most other women do in wartime, she agonized, worked, worried, exulted, and worked again. Both sides at the beginning thought that there would be a brief glorious campaign and then victory. Not until months had gone by, and defeat, bereavement, and destruction had begun to come home to every person, did both sides learn what war really is.

The great outpouring of patriotism by all people alike was an extraordinary stimulus to a person of Louisa's character. She had always had a deep feeling on the subject of slavery. The terror-stricken runaway concealed in the big brick oven had haunted her memory ever since early childhood. Nor had her warmly grateful heart ever forgotten the unknown Negro boy who had snatched her out of the Frog Pond when she was drowning. To her it was a glorious chance now to fling herself into work which was to help save these oppressed people and to free America from the fruit of its most terrible mistake. It was a tremendous experience to know that thousands were feeling the same thing and that all were pressing forward to achieve the same high end. She understood all sorts of people; she was interested in them and she had occasion to know and to study every kind of woman as they all toiled together at sewing, scraping lint, and preparing bandages. But the most of what she got out of this work and out of the greater things which she did later was the knowledge that here at last was a vent for her long-burning sense of injustice, kindled on that astounding day when she was such a little girl and had seen the fugitive hidden in the oven.

She was teaching again that first winter of the war, for Miss Elizabeth Peabody was starting kindergartens here and there and urged that Louisa take charge of one just opening in the Warren Street Chapel. She did not accept the task willingly and was glad when it came to an end. It is worth remembering; for it was the last time that she ever taught. A queer little incident is recorded at this time. There was a great memorial meeting for John Brown, hero of Harper's Ferry, whose soul went marching on through the battle songs of that terrible struggle. Louisa could not go to that meeting, as she wrote in her journal, "because she had no good gown." Cousin Lizzie Wells' silk dress had evidently come to the last of its days. But poor John Brown, in his butternut coat; why could Louisa not do reverence to his memory in her shabby garments of every day? War had not yet broken down some odd restrictions, which had stood too long. Louisa wrote a poem, however, which was read aloud to thousands in the solemn quiet of that great assemblage. Her real poems have been very few, put forward shyly at times of great feeling.

The first twelve months dragged slowly toward their end. There had been no very glorious campaigns; most of the victories had been on the side of the South. Battles had been fought, hospitals were filling up with wounded and with the hosts of sick, which war brings in its train. There was greater and greater call for nurses. Louisa had seen the home soldiers march away, down the Lexington and Concord road, past the gray stone walls behind which the fighting men of another war had taken cover, past the pink-blossomed apple trees. The flags were waving, the fifes were playing "The Girl I Left Behind Me," the drums were thumping, beating on the very hearts of those who saw them go. There is no experience in the world that can ever match that of seeing soldiers go away, of seeing the gaiety and the excitement, and of knowing the black and hopeless tragedy which is behind it all. There is little that is so terrible as seeing strong wholesome young men, every one of them beautiful in the flush of their high patriotism, as watching them go and knowing that they are surely to die.

Louisa had all the desperate emotion which goes with such a sight; but the most of what she felt consciously was a frantic desire to go also. As the weeks passed and then the months, she knew that this excited wish had grown into steady resolve. Would it be fair, she wondered, to give up for a while her own battle for the security and happiness of her family? This was a time when there was no thought of security and happiness for anyone; there cannot be during a war. She was young, she was very strong, she was a good nurse, as all of her family testified. Elizabeth had loved her ministrations more than those of anyone else; Cousin Lizzie Wells was loud in her praises of Louisa's care, which had brought her through a difficult illness; Abba Alcott could bear witness to the same thing. Louisa's nursing was vigorous and hopeful, cheerful and sympathetic, and had the background of a good deal of experience. It was plain that there was need for just such a person as herself. In November she sent in her application, hardly knowing at just what moment she had come to the final decision.

She went about the house making her preparations, packing her clothes, doing last sewing for her family that they might not miss her too much while she was gone. "Will I ever come back?" was the question which repeated itself over and over within her mind. She was facing heavy work, hardship, and great danger from the pestilence and infections with which the hospitals were filled. But she knew that she could not resist longer.

"The blood of the Mays is up," she announced. If someone questioned her or protested, she answered only, "I must go."

# CHAPTER SIX

❧ ❧ ❧

## Kit

THE CITY OF WASHINGTON LAY SILENT IN the raw cold of a cloudy December day, silent and listening. It was almost as if the people walking to and fro in the broad streets were afraid to speak aloud; it was as though they were all straining their ears for a sound just too far off to be actually heard. A great battle was going forward. That was official news brought to the tall, gaunt man in the White House, who was even now walking up and down the long office room, waiting and listening just as was everyone else. Rumors were flocking in — General Burnside, the Union commander, was splendidly victorious — General Burnside was in utter rout with all his forces. Rumors of a battle always contradict one another for a little while, until finally the truth comes drifting in. The truth came at last. It was news of a signal defeat of the Union troops at Fredericksburg. Close behind it came the rumble of heavy wheels as the ambulances brought thousands of wounded to the hospitals of Washington.

Louisa Alcott's new life as a nurse had just begun. She had not learned very much about her duties as yet, only which ward was to be hers, how the meals of fat pork and dish-water coffee were served, how many different people must be applied to before an order for bandages and medicine could be filled. The hospital to which she had been sent was in Georgetown, on high ground just outside Washington. The building had once been a large hotel, wherein slatternly housekeeping with lazy, casual servants had held sway for years. Upon the accumulation of dirt and dilapidation there had been poured the hastily gathered equipment of a hospital — flimsy iron cots, dingy mattresses, hard pillows, bedding and crockery and surgeons' supplies in all the necessary enormous quantities.

It had looked, nevertheless, like an imposing place to Louisa as she drove up in the dark, saw the rows of lighted windows and the guards at the door. The recollection of her travels was still like a great adventure upon her, so unused was she to even so modestly brief a journey at this. May and Julian to see her off in Concord, the night spent in Boston with Cousin Lizzie Wells, a few last pangs of wonder and foreboding, then Anna and John Pratt saying good-bye before the puffing train bore her southward! To go from Boston to Washington was an elaborate process in 1862; one journeyed by train to New London, by boat to New York, took another inexpressibly early train from Jersey City, and reached Washington long after dark. She had studied her traveling companions with edification; she had chuckled delightedly over the tribulations of hoop-skirted ladies trying to go to bed in the narrow cabin berth of the steamer.

As Philadelphia went past the car windows she pressed her nose to the pane and wished that she could stop a little to see more of her "native city." When she came at last to her journey's end, was carried in a bumping cab over the long drive to Georgetown, and when she finally dismounted, stiff with lengthy uncomfortable traveling, the first sensation which came over her was a wave of terrific shyness. All these strange people, a crowd of men about the door — how was she to face them; what was she supposed to do first? She walked forward boldly, was admitted, welcomed, and taken to her room.

A tiny apartment it was, for which the words bare and dreary would give too rich a description. Two inhospitable iron beds told her that she was to share it with another nurse. Half the window panes were broken, and opposite the curtainless opening the innumerable windows of a great hospital in a church across the way stared in upon her. It was inadequately warmed by a narrow fireplace in which a pair of bricks supported one end of a log, which, too big for the aperture, extended out into the room and had to be pushed into the fireplace by degrees as the wood burned away. The closet was tiny, full of cockroaches, and loud with the scampering of rats. She was warned at once to leave nothing of value lying about, as the hospital attendants were rapacious thieves.

When she was introduced to her duties in the ward she looked about in dismay at the rows of sagging beds, the dirty floors, the unwashed windows, and the long corridors haunted with evil smells. The comfortable, plain neatness of the house in Concord seemed a thing of which she had dreamed, so remote it appeared to be from this vast dismal place. But she had come to work and, no matter what the circumstances were, work she would do. There was no lack of it. A nurse had just given out, ill, and her place was thrust upon Louisa, so that with no training and with insufficient knowledge she found herself immediately superintendent of a ward containing forty beds. Those who occupied them were suffering variously from measles, diphtheria, and typhoid.

The hospital nevertheless was not crowded just then; most of the patients were recovering to a certain degree, so that the pressure for the first three days was not unendurable. She began to get acquainted with her fellow workers, with the faces on the pillows, faces which very soon learned to brighten as she came near. Even without surgical skill or proper knowledge Louisa was a rare nurse. She might be shy, weary, or sick at heart, but even here she always remained good company.

Like the others, she had waited through the long dark day for news from Fredericksburg and had gone to bed, worn out with apprehension. At three o'clock in the morning she was awakened by the general summons —

"The wounded are coming."

They came streaming in, filling every vacant bed and cot, waiting in the halls, laid on pallets on the floor. Those who could walk stood in dismal groups about the stoves, cold, wet, and dirty. They had been fighting in the rain and mud for three days, and when they were hurt were bundled into the ambulances with only the briefest of emergency treatment. Louisa, who thought that she was used to sickness and nursing, had no experience of anything like this.

"What do I do first?" she asked desperately of a superior hurrying past.

"Wash them," was the brief reply.

So, armed with a tin basin, a towel so rough that it might be made of sandpaper, and a cake of brown soap which at home she would have used only for scrubbing the floor, she advanced upon her task. She began with the man in the bed nearest her, a person so covered with dirt that his own family might not have known him. She commenced to draw off his ragged uniform, working easily and gently as she knew how to do, holding her breath for fear a groan of pain would reproach her efforts.

"May your bed above be aisy, darlin', for the day's work you are doin'," said a rich, cheerful voice. Louisa, hearing it, laughed aloud with relief. Faces on the long row of pillows turned and smiled and the Irish soldier laughed with her. It was a good beginning.

During the first days and nights which followed she was nothing but a bundle of tired aches, driven somehow by a determined will and a cool head. How much there was to do and what aimless confusion and lack of management there were to hinder the doing of it! There were calls for her in every direction and need for help even amongst those who had no strength to call. At first all these gray worn faces looked alike to her; but little by little she began to know her horde of new patients, the cheery Irishman, the querulous, complaining man with a little wound, the big, patient Virginia blacksmith with a mortal one. It was on her first turn of night duty that she became acquainted with the little drummer boy and his friend, Kit.

As she walked between the beds through the great candlelit cave which had once been the hotel ballroom, she caught the noise of a stifled crying, a strange sound in that heroic company where even groans were comparatively rare. In the last bed was the smallest patient in the hospital, Billy, the drummer boy, aged only twelve. As Louisa bent over him, he broke into open, little-boy weeping.

"I dreamed that Kit was here and when I waked up he wasn't." He shook with sobs, as well as with the terrific chill which had waked him.

She quieted him as only Louisa really could have known how to do and presently got his story from him, spoken softly lest the rest of the ward be disturbed. The yellow candle shone down upon his white, drawn, pitifully small face as he looked up at her and told her everything that had happened. Men were so badly needed in the army that the Government was obliged to accept boys to beat the rolling drums and blow the bugles. Billy had been the object of envy of all his young friends when he marched away with the regiment, thumping gloriously as they went down the road. He had drummed for long weary marches in the hot sun, in the rain and the snow; he had never lagged though his legs were short and his strength only half that of a real soldier's. He fell ill with fever during the Fredericksburg campaign and was burning and shivering in his tent when the command came to go into battle.

He lay under the wavering canvas, hearkening to the boom of the guns, hearing the cheer of his comrades as they went into action. He could not move, he could only wait and wonder. He thought of each one whom he knew, the one who liked to tease him, the one who gave him good advice, and Kit, splendid Kit, who was his chief friend and the object of his adoration. Would the battle bring harm to Kit? That was his chief thought as he lay there and watched the tent canvas shiver and tremble in the cold wind.

What was this he heard now, the sound of feet, thousands of feet going by the tent, not with measured tread of marching, but with haste, with running panic?

"Was this a retreat? Could it possibly be that Kit — that General Burnside's army — had been forced back by the Johnny Rebs?"

There was a voice at the tent door. Someone was standing against the light. It was Kit with the kindly face and the strong arms who gathered him up from his bed of blankets on the ground. Too weak to ask questions, Billy lay against his friend's shoulder and was carried away in the vast, dreary river of defeat which flowed down all the roads that led from Fredericksburg.

More than one voice said near them, "You're hurt yourself, Kit; let me take him."

But his comrade would not give him up. The endless shuffle of weary feet changed finally to the rumble of ambulance wheels but still the two traveled on, still Kit's arm was around him. Billy fell into a long sleep of complete exhaustion and wakened only at the hospital door. He was being lifted, but by whose hands? Where was Kit? A battered soldier near him told him as gently as he could that Kit had — had gone. Billy would have cried out in anguish, but soldiers did not do that. He was one of the regiment; he must take this blow without whimpering. He did.

In the hospital he lay silent and wide-eyed, facing his grief with unwavering spirit. It was the dream which betrayed him. He dreamed that Kit was with him again, that they were sitting together by the bivouac fire, laughing and joking as they had so often done. Kit's warm hand was on his shoulder, his strong voice was speaking just beside him — and suddenly he awoke to the shadowy ward, to the flickering lights from the candles and the glowing stove, to the rows of silent beds. Grief took him unawares and he wept, stifling the great sobs in the pillow as best he could. It was so that Louisa found him. It was into her ear that he poured out the whole story. For a whole hour she listened and comforted. At last he was cheered and quieted; at last he was dropping to sleep.

Louisa leaned back in her chair to rest a minute and draw her breath; for it had taken all her strength and spirit to help the desolate little boy. How tired she was and how long the night! But she could be still for a little now, she thought, and gather courage again.

A step behind her made her start and turn about. A long rifleman from Pennsylvania had risen from his bed and was tramping down the ward, walking in the sleep of pain-ridden fever. She rushed to him and seized him by the arm, protesting and commanding. It was dangerous for him to be walking about with a serious wound; he must get back to bed at once.

"I'm going home," he announced, and tramped on. He would neither wake nor listen. Tall Louisa hanging on his arm was as nothing to his gigantic strength as he strode onward, repeating steadily, "I'm going home."

A huge fellow at the end of the ward, less seriously hurt than some of the others, rose from his blankets and came to her rescue. His powerful arms accomplished what her remonstrances could not; so that finally he led the wanderer back to his own place. Quiet settled down again; Billy was asleep, the lank Pennsylvanian was drifting into more peaceful dreams, muttering still now and then that he was going home.

That was what they all dreamed about in that crowded, ill-smelling place — home. Louisa knew it, for her own thoughts at the back of her mind were always on the clean perfume of pine-covered hills, on the glint of the river between green meadows, on the lighted windows in the friendly houses all along the road.

In the brief free hour between the night watch and the day she wrote letters to her family of whom she thought so incessantly. The place that she was in was squalid and dreary; there was no romance in the sights she was seeing now, so she thought. But she was bound that they at home should see it all, just as she was always seeing them in the inner vision of her mind. As the days went by she wrote and wrote whenever she could snatch a minute, so that they too would become acquainted with the blacksmith John Sulie and jolly little Sergeant Bain, with Billy and Kit. She herself had learned to know Kit as well as though he were actually there, even though the knowledge came entirely through the chatter of Billy who had taken her for his confidante. She was often so tired that the writing wavered on the page; but the picture that she drew in words was always clear.

She did not feel as strong and undaunted as she had intended to be. Although she did not know it she was actually perishing for want of the fresh, bracing air which she had always breathed, of the spare, wholesome food which she was used to eating. She could have courage to steel her heart against the onslaughts of homesickness and the sight of suffering all about; but she could not steel her body against the poisons of that unhealthy place. She grew daily more thin and pale, but everyone around her was far too busy to notice such a thing.

In spite of all she felt, Louisa could be nothing other than herself. The ward which she had in charge resounded with laughter just as the old house in Concord had done. Here was suffering everywhere; but there were jokes everywhere also, since there is no place where something comic cannot be discovered. Some people thought the mirth unseemly; but the men laughed and loved her. The windows were nailed down; but she wrenched them loose and threw them open for a time every day, quite deaf to the dire prophecies of what the consequences might be. She made beds, carried trays, and dressed wounds, and left her patients chuckling whenever she turned away to a new task. How she managed it she could not have told anyone. She did it by being Louisa.

While she was on night duty she slept half the day and spent the other half going about Washington. She knew that she must have some fresh air and in spite of weariness always managed to find enough enterprise for roaming abroad. She had seen so little of the world that she felt she must make the most of this chance. Washington in wartime was a strange, crowded, thrilling place. The endless lines of army wagons crawled through the streets, each drawn by its team of six mules. Louisa loved animals and found mules fascinating, they were so unfamiliar and so extraordinarily clever. She would see an astute old beast, tired of pulling, deliberately lie down in the street, as though to die, straightway bringing about a traffic jam of profane and enraged proportions. A crowd would gather; remedies would be applied, strong remedies such as mule drivers know. The big, black animal would lie inert, evidently come to the last of his pulling. Everyone would offer advice; the other mules would stand patiently waiting, watching their fallen comrade with expressions of mild reproach and surprise. At last, after blocking the activities of the United States Government for half an hour, the recumbent mule would change his mind, arise with awkward scramblings, and go cheerfully on his way as though no small unpleasantness of any kind had occurred.

The streets were filled with strolling soldiers garbed in the bright parti-colored uniforms which have no place in war of the present day, white breeches, red fezzes, gold embroidered coats, little blue jackets which swung over the shoulders. Different regiments had different costumes, each vying with the other for brilliant effect. There would be columns of marching troops in blue-gray, caped overcoats, rifles on shoulders, faces set and grim with the memory of what the men had so recently seen. If she did not see him herself she heard people talking everywhere of the President who used to go about Washington on horseback, amidst all this hurry and bustle, incongruously dressed in his long black coat, black, ill-fitting trousers, and tall hat, a queer, ungainly figure against the background of all this pomp and circumstance of war. The guard which he was forced to have and to which he was so indifferent would come clattering behind, very magnificent, to make up for the shabbiness of that tall man with the dark, lined, deeply absorbed face who rode ahead.

She visited the Capitol, finding it of special

interest for a fantastic reason. She had seen a picture of it when she was small and had always in her mind's eye taken it for the model of a fairy palace. Cinderella, so she imagined, went to housekeeping with the Prince, after the glass slipper episode, in just such a mansion. She climbed the broad stairs and went in — to be greatly disillusioned. It was big and impressive; but to her eyes there was no romance here. Congress was not sitting nor the Senate, so that the place was given over to janitors who stood about and gossiped and idly plied here and there an intermittent broom. There was an unexpected smell of fresh bread through the whole building from the huge bakery in the cellar where loaves were baked for the troops stationed about Washington. The crowded streets were more interesting, where through the mud or the dust or the snow and amid the casual groups of strolling pigs, there toiled ever forward the long, picturesque, relentless procession of the war.

She was changed finally to day duty where the routine went on always in set order and always with infinite variations. Breakfast came first, with its innumerable trays and teapots, then bed-making, then the dressing of wounds. There would be no bandages; she would rush all over the building to get an order signed for more. Adhesive tape would be lacking; the orderly who had charge of the supplies would have to be found, would be discovered after long search, drunk in the lower regions, and would have to be told in no uncertain terms to return to his duty. Stouthearted Louisa could perform this part of her office rather well and the man would go shambling back to his place with promises of no further backsliding. Some patients would get better, would begin to be spoiled and demand incessant attention; some would be worse and have to be watched over constantly. One woman came every day to see her husband who, as everyone knew but herself, had not long to live. He passed in the night so suddenly that no one had time to send warning to her, and she came in to see him just as usual in the morning.

"Why, where's Emanuel?" she cried out in terror, as she saw the empty cot. Men turned their heads, nurses stood still; who was to tell her? The limping Irish orderly came up and took her gently by the arm.

"Sure, they've moved him to a better bed. Come with me, dear, while I show you." And he led her away.

There were a few others who were regular visitors and one woman who insisted against all the rules on staying to care for her sick son. She was a thorn in the flesh of the hospital staff; for her sharp scolding voice could be heard all day, finding fault of every kind with institution and nurses, food, and management, since nothing afforded proper service for George. In spite of her small-spirited complaining, however, she showed courage and indefatigable devotion. There was no bed for her, so she slept upon the floor beside her boy's cot and rose up in the morning more acid and irritable than before. The men made all manner of game of her, some of it of no delicate nature, but she paid no attention and continued with her ministrations. She did some good, for she was a constant joke in the ward; she was an example, though rather an odd one, of persevering loyalty. It was with mixed feelings that they all saw her gather up the convalescent George finally and take him elsewhere. The ward was more peaceful after she was gone; but there was something missing which had been of use at least to break the monotony of the days.

A languishing lady came to volunteer her services for taking care of the dear boys and was put through a severe catechism within Louisa's hearing. Could she work hard? No, she was always greatly fatigued after an hour or two of effort. Did she find it easy to keep awake at night? Oh, dear, she could not do night duty, she was afraid to watch alone, and was all in a tremble at the very thought of a delirious patient.

Could she help dress wounds and bathe feverish patients? No, she was very much afraid of infection. She also dropped the fact that she fainted at the sight of blood. There could be little hope that she could eat the food, the salt beef, the bread which seemed to be made of straw and sawdust, the sloppy coffee. Her services were not accepted.

There was one man of whom the others talked much even before he arrived. It was John Sulie, the giant blacksmith from Virginia. His comrades on the battlefield all told of how John had insisted that others be picked up and cared for before himself, and so did not come with the first consignment of wounded. They wondered and worried lest he should not be brought to the same place. Louisa went in to look at him asleep the evening after he finally arrived, a man so tall that his bed had to be lengthened to hold him. His face was splendid and serene, "like a great statesman's," she said afterward. She came to know him well; for her presence seemed to help him bear the pain of having his wounds dressed. He was tremendously strong, with a body which had been magnificent before the shells of war had torn it almost to pieces. The surgeon in charge took Louisa aside and laid a duty upon her. It was she who, when the time came, must tell this man that he was to die.

She did. A nurse must do as she is told. She sat beside him, wrote his last letters to that family which he had been supporting before the conviction came upon him that he must go to war. A mother, a younger brother, and sisters — he was taking care of them all. The young brother would have to do it now. He dictated the messages and as she wrote them down, said only to her, "I hope the answer will come in time for me to see it."

They called her in the night to tell her that he was going and that he wanted her. She stood by while his dearest comrade of march and battle and campfire said good-bye to him. War makes some terrible things and some beautiful ones; the most beautiful is the regard of one hard, scarred soldier for another. She felt that she also had lost a beloved friend when suffering at last relaxed its hold and let him go.

She made other friends; she could not fail to make many in this strangely assorted company. One was little Sergeant Bain who was apt to get into mischief in the ward, like an idle small boy. His right arm was disabled, but he insisted on writing certain letters himself with his left hand, blushing all the while and beginning them, as she could not help seeing, "My dearest Jane." She heard all about Jane finally and nursed that young lady's adorer back to sufficient health for him to go home to lay his heart before her. She used to tell him stories out of Dickens when the pain was unendurable, and he could always laugh. There was a big German of elaborate manners and enormous heart, who was a great help to her in the ward, who comforted Billy when he was longing for Kit. Billy got well, the German got well, many got well and went away. All of them bade her the most grateful of good-byes. Some of them kissed her.

In spite of all the good that she was doing, things were not going well with Louisa. That feeble lady who admitted to fainting at the sight of blood was right in one thing, impotent and silly as she was. She did well to be afraid of infection. It was everywhere in that crowded, unclean place. The vile smells proclaimed it, the close air, the dirt-sodden floors and the dingy walls. With no respect for persons, it attacked the sick and the wounded, the nurses and the doctors alike. On the first day that she came, Louisa had cared for measles, diphtheria, typhoid, and pneumonia, all in the same room. She was put in charge of her first ward because another nurse "had been taken ill." Louisa presently developed such a cold that it seemed as though she were to have pneumonia. That, however, was merely by the way. What she did have was typhoid.

The illness came on slowly. Her feet became heavier and heavier; she coughed so that she had to stop and hold to things until the paroxysm was over. She took a walk one day up to the Georgetown Heights above the hospital where there were woods and paths and a far view over the Potomac. She stood beside a clear, bright-running brook and could hardly believe that this peace and beauty were so near to all that was crowded with pain and terror. It was the last time that she walked abroad. The next day was cold and stormy and her own strength was at an end. The doctors at last took notice of her state and ordered her to keep her room.

Even now she was not willing to give in. She sat at the window, sewing and writing her letters home. She still wanted those at home to know of the further fortunes of John and the Sergeant and Billy. Most of all she seemed to want them to understand about Kit, whom she had never seen. He had died at the hospital door, but he seemed, nonetheless, to be the real hero of all that heroic company. She did not speak of how ill she was.

Although the weeks had seemed so full and so long she had only been at the hospital a little more than a month. The first of January passed and with it a tremendous event. Back in September, Abraham Lincoln, amid much criticism and a storm of protest, had issued his preliminary Emancipation Proclamation, declaring that when the New Year began all slaves in the United States should be "forever free." Louisa saw that "forever" begin. With the stroke of midnight freedom descended upon those thousands who had never dreamed of anything but toiling servitude. Bells rang, jubilant Negroes marched through the streets, shouting, weeping, singing "Glory Hallelujah." Louisa flung up her window and leaned out to cheer with the rest. The face of that fugitive, of whom she had thought ever since her childhood, was a ghost in her memory which could now be laid — forever.

She became more and more ill and finally could not rise from her bed. Her room was cold and raw, with the chill and fog coming in through the broken windows. She could hear rats scurrying in the wall, while all the evil smells of the vast, unsanitary place came pouring in upon her. She lay there thinking about the work which she could do no more, about the hospital days, about the barren Sundays. Occasionally a dull uninterested chaplain preached a hurried sermon to men, every one of them in need of religion, some of them on the edge of eternity, all of them with hearts opened by pain and the ghastly memories of battle. What would it be, she wondered, if Theodore Parker should suddenly be there; how would his strong voice sound ringing through the crowded, pain-filled room; what if his great knowledge of God could minister to these groping ones? Theodore Parker had been dead nearly three years; but she knew, still, every word he had ever said to help her in her own need. He had given her courage to face some hard things; she could face this.

One night she woke suddenly, coughing and cold to the very bones. If the fire had gone completely out she was helpless to rekindle it. The chilliness meant much misery; perhaps it might even mean death. She sat up in bed and saw a figure kneeling before the fireplace. It was the surgeon, busy and hard-worked all day, but come now to see that she was safe. He had brought an armload of kindling, which he had split himself downstairs and was whittling shavings for fuel to start the dead fire. He looked about and saw her sitting up against the thin pillow with the inadequate blankets wrapped about her.

"You will have to go home," he asserted peremptorily.

She shook her head. She had enlisted for three months; she could not give up after only one. She hardly remembered now how she had nursed as her first cases men with typhoid in that stifling and dirty place. The matron of the hospital was ill with typhoid also, was thought to be at the point of death, although Louisa did not know it. The Mays were an obstinate race. Louisa would not go. But home — beautiful and delicious word. She lay down and went to sleep thinking of it.

A week later she heard that word spoken again. The world around her was a dizzy blur now, through which figures came and went, tending her, unendingly bringing her food which she could not eat and water which she could not drink. The matron had issued from her bed the peremptory order that Miss Alcott must be taken where she could have better care. Suddenly to Louisa's bewildered surprise a face leaned over her, a thin, fine-cut countenance which, even now, had not lost its look of peaceful and serene dignity. How could her father possibly be there? But it surely was he; this was his own voice saying:

"I have come to take you home."

Even now she still refused to go, held by the unreasonable obstinacy of illness. For five days Bronson stayed and nursed her. He was a good nurse, with an inexhaustible fund of gentleness and untroubled patience. It did not seem wise to take Louisa away against her will.

She tossed and fretted and worried over the work which she had come to do, which now must go on without her. The men would miss her, she lamented. Just when she had come to know how best to take care of them, she had surrendered to weakness. Another matter troubled her. There was a rule of the hospital that the rough work of the wards was done by such men as were enough recovered to be up and about. With the lack of system and of any wise management, these convalescents were often ordered to do totally improper tasks. The nurses who had labored to get the wounded really set upon the road to recovery could not endure seeing their good work undone by some blundering order which laid upon a half-well man labor far too hard for him. One soldier, with such a bad heart that he should never have been taken into the army at all, was given heavy trays to carry, made to lift ponderous, helpless men until the work brought him suddenly into far worse illness than that with which he had first come. Another young boy, with a badly injured back, was put to the duty of scrubbing floors, in spite of the visible agony which it cost him. When this injustice was practiced in her ward, Louisa had a simple remedy. She herself lifted and carried and got down on her knees to scrub the floor, often after twelve hours of intensive, all-night duty. As she lay helpless, however, she worried continually over these unfortunates and feared no one would care for them. The days passed;

the matron of the hospital, ill with the same malady, died. At last Louisa was too weak to resist longer and they prepared to take her away.

Everyone came out to see her go, her fellow nurses with comforts, the "boys" with small presents, a head nurse with a shawl, a Bible, and a final list of sharp, imperious admonitions such as had been, for Louisa, a source of mirth and despair ever since she came. All of what was going on about her was nothing to Louisa now, as she was taken down to the waiting carriage, was accompanied to the station by a crowd of friends and was got somehow upon the train. It is probable that Bronson remembered that journey, every hour of it, as long as he lived, but upon Louisa it made no impression. Occasionally she would rouse herself to see faces staring at her, curious, or shocked, or horrified countenances, taking in her dishevelled hair, her flushed cheeks, and her rumpled clothes. There was a pause and some uncomfortable changing about; that was Boston. Another effort followed, a sight of an agonized, terrified face which looked like her mother's, then a bed, a comfortable bed with cool sheets and a white soft pillow, upon which she could at last lay down her aching head. This was home.

# CHAPTER SEVEN

❧❧ ❧❧ ❧❧

## "Thoreau's Flute"

IN HER ROOM LOOKING OUT ABOVE THE LEX-
ington and Concord highway, Louisa lay for
weeks, wrapped in the cloud of delirium, hearing vaguely the sounds which came up from
without, as the long battle went on within. She
heard sleigh bells at first, then crows cawing,
then robins singing. The fields were all white
with deep drifts the day that she was brought
into the house; the Mayflowers were in bloom
on the hillside the morning when she came
weakly to the door again and looked abroad
upon the world. Thin, shaky, and with shorn
hair, she was scarcely recognizable even to herself when she looked into the glass. Her homecoming, that staggering walk to the door, and
the days between were like a bad dream; but
they were over. She need never think of them
again.

Two things of importance had happened in
that interval. One was an intensely happy event
of a domestic nature. Bronson Alcott, one cold,

161

wet day in March, came down from Boston, making something in the nature of a triumphal progress. He had a piece of news to tell which he communicated at once to the stage driver, as he climbed into the creaking coach.

"I am a grandfather. Anna has a son."

The driver, an old acquaintance, was delighted, and congratulated him warmly upon his honors. Such of his fellow passengers as he knew, and he knew most of them, were also favored with the splendid intelligence. As he dismounted from the stage to walk home he met Mr. Emerson. It was glorious to be able to tell his old friend these good tidings, "Anna has a fine boy." He could not stop long to discuss the great event, however, since those at home, at Orchard House, did not yet know of it. He burst in, waving his umbrella, wet with the rain and snow, shining with joy as he announced, "Anna has a boy."

He was met, as is usual on such occasions, by a chorus of delighted feminine outcry, so that he could scarcely complete the announcement with the proper formula, "Mother and child both doing well." Mrs. Alcott shed tears, May gloated, Louisa exclaimed in indignation that she had been defrauded, and where was her namesake, Louisa Caroline?

Decision was immediately made that Mrs.

162

Alcott should go to visit the baby and that May could manage the housekeeping while she was gone. This being March, Louisa was just barely beginning to sit up. Her hair had commenced to grow again, making short curls all about her head. Although she had no trace of vanity, she had sadly discovered one weak point in her nature. She was almost inconsolable over the loss of her hair. "My one beauty," she had always described it. No light vow was it — that which she had made when she was so much younger — that if the family fortunes did not mend, she would sell her hair. Now, after some real lamentation, she declared that though she had not been able to lay down her life for her country, fortune had deigned to accept the patriotic sacrifice of her hair. With this thought she began to be comforted.

It was a tonic to her to feel and to share the joy over "Anna's angel," as they fell to calling the baby. Through all of Louisa's illness, her mother had been so anxious; her father Louisa described as being completely worn out with taking care of her. Either her father or her mother had been with her every minute of the weeks when she lay so near to death. Now the whole household took on a different, a triumphant tone, as it talked and exulted over the arrival of the new member of the family, for whom Louisa, since

Louisa Caroline was not to be an appropriate title, had suggested the name of Amos Minot Bridge Bronson May Sewall Alcott Pratt. It can be seen that the family connection was large and loyal. In the end, a compromise was made and the baby was called Frederic Alcott Pratt.

Louisa's first activity was a little sewing for this most wonderful of all babies. She was still really ill, since all her powers were so completely gone that it was to take a very long time to recover them. So weak and worn out was she that she had not even the spirit to be impatient, but moved feebly about, managing to be busy by the hour at small tasks which she would once have tossed aside in five energetic minutes. By April, she was able to drive and even walk a little in the garden and along the road under the apple trees.

The family's dear friend, Henry Thoreau, had died during the winter. In one of the rare quiet hours of her night watching at the hospital, Louisa had composed some lines on the death of this shy genius whom they all loved so dearly. In the stress of what came later, she forgot them; but now, as she began to awake to real living and thinking, they came back to her. She wrote them down, but showed them to nobody.

As has been said, the old Hillside house, not far from the dwelling of the Alcotts, belonged to the Hawthornes, long-standing friends of theirs, as well as of Thoreau's. Julian Hawthorne tells of a warm summer evening when, as they sat inside, they heard light steps on the porch and a rustle at the door. No one knocked or rang the bell, so they sat for a few minutes, wondering who might be there. On his going to the door, finally, he found a folded paper thrust under the crack and no person in sight. He brought it in to his father, Nathaniel Hawthorne, and they opened it together. It was Louisa's poem on "Thoreau's Flute," which she wanted them to see but was too shy to bring openly. She always made verses rather freely, but this vein of real poetry was rarely touched and only on occasions when some great feeling had stirred her. The last was upon the death of John Brown.

A little later Mrs. Hawthorne showed the lines to the editor of the *Atlantic*, who published them as a tribute to the man for whom all of them were mourning. After the magazine came out, Bronson Alcott was one day in the study of his friend, Henry Wadsworth Longfellow, at Cambridge.

"Just see," said Longfellow, getting out the *Atlantic*, in which contributions at that time were published without names, "I want you to read this poem by Emerson on Thoreau."

"Louisa wrote that," returned Bronson, in a fine glow of fatherly pride. Emerson, at that time, was thought to be one of the foremost writers in America, so that Bronson's pleasure was excusable. It is no wonder that some of Louisa's best work resembled Emerson's — had he not taught her much of what she knew? She said once that she owed most of her education to these two men, Emerson and Theodore Parker.

The second event of importance which had come about while she was ill had to do with her writing. Her letters home had been so interesting that, while she was still at the hospital, extracts were shown to Mr. Frank B. Sanborn, who was editor of a paper called the *Commonwealth.* He was so much impressed by what Louisa had written that he straightway put the letters into print, with the title "Hospital Sketches." Kit and Billy, John Sulie and Sergeant Bain became familar figures to many besides the immediate Alcott family. Everyone, at just that time, wanted to know about the hospitals and how fathers and brothers would fare if taken there. Louisa had told of the life with extraordinary effect; for she was not straining after romance now, but had given the truth simply, graphically, and with great spirit. The jokes were made more of than the pathos; the courage more than the suffering. She had managed to make each man stand out, nevertheless. Kit most of all. Kit, whom she knew only through Billy's tearful story, had brought her first real success. People were reading "Hospital Sketches" everywhere, and the *Commonwealth* was asking for more.

Her family told Louisa of all this while she was still too ill really to understand it. Her mind was too weak to take in such news and she simply did not believe it. That she should be turning out to be a real writer, the sort of writer of whom people talked and for whose work they clamored, that could never be. She was only worn-out Louisa Alcott, a total failure. When she got a little better, however, she thought more about the strange news. It could hardly be true, yet it was pleasant to credit it, just for a little while. She had no feeling that she ever wanted to write again. But presently, as she became stronger still, and as the requests for more of "Hospital Sketches" were unceasing, she made the effort to complete them, to tell all she knew about her friends, the cheery Irishman and Sergeant Bain and big German Fritz. She wanted people to understand fully that all the heroism was not on the battlefield.

The war dragged on with the long, depressing, indeterminate campaigns on both sides. She could read the papers and see in the accounts what others did not; she could picture how, after each battle, the wounded would come streaming in, tired, unfed, untended, each man with his own suffering and his own need. How hard it was that she should not be there to do what she, at such cost, had learned how to do! At first, she said that when she got better she would apply for a place in the hospital again, this time in one of the newly formed establishments for black regiments. She had not forgotten her strong partisanship of the Negroes.

She had been a little astonished at first when she saw in Washington what seemed to her a very different sort of black people from those hard-working, thrifty souls who had accomplished their freedom and established residence in the North. These seemingly lighthearted children of bondage were something very new to her experience. She would look at the small army of serving women who came into the hospital in the morning, some big and slatternly, some little and trim; several, usually, with a child or two hanging at their skirts; all of them gay and laughing and friendly. All day there would come up from the laundry in the basement the smell of steam and soapsuds and the unending clatter of cheerful talk. There were small children who ran errands in the hospital, up and down the stairs or from building to building, the Civil War substitute for the telephone system. They would steal anything the moment the owner's back was turned, but they were always cheerily obliging and good-natured. She was not shocked by any of them and grew to feel that, novel as they were to her, she understood them.

When she realized finally that she would never be strong enough for nursing again, she had another plan. She took up the idea of volunteering to teach in one of the schools which the Government was organizing for contrabands, as the freed Negroes were coming to be called. But once more she was obliged to admit that she was still powerless to carry out any such purpose. The lowering, hovering anxiety which war brings and from which no one could ever escape in those dark days did not make an atmosphere in which it was easy to get well.

There is something about war which makes people feel that it is going to last forever. Four years — was it true that it had only been that much, when it seemed so like a half a lifetime? It seemed scarcely possible to think what the days would be without torturing suspense, without continual dread of bad news. It was not within the power of anyone's imagination to picture troops marching home, hundreds of them, whole and safe, instead of marching away to that imminent prospect of violent death. But yet the impossible finally happens. There came news of the surrender at Appomattox, and the nightmare was over. The men were coming home.

They came marching down the Lexington road on a hot afternoon, the drums beating with a different message, the flags flying to the wind of victory. The very sound of their feet was triumphant happiness, even though the tramp was muffled in the thick dust. Everyone turned out to see them come. The young Hawthornes ran over to the Orchard House as a better point of vantage to see them pass. The Alcotts had prepared gallons of lemonade and gigantic supplies of plum cake. The tired, thirsty soldiers were allowed to fall out before the gate and were royally entertained. Louisa stood talking to the captain, as two veterans will, comparing war experiences and discussing common acquaintances. The afternoon sun was getting low when finally the command was given to fall in and march onward. The last glass of lemonade was hastily swallowed, the last thanks were stammered, as the men hurried out into the road. Louisa stood at the gate to watch them go. Suddenly, just as they were all in line and ready to march away, a cheer broke out, which lifted and rang and echoed against the wooded hill — a cheer for Louisa. These men, too, knew that not all the heroism had been found on the battlefield.

They tramped away wrapped in a cloud of sunlit golden dust and Julian Hawthorne came up to speak to Louisa. He fell back abruptly. Not in all his life before had he seen tears on Louisa's face; even her family had seen her weep on only the rarest of occasions. But she was weeping now as she turned away and walked into the house.

Upon a person of Louisa's nature the assassination of Abraham Lincoln was bound to make a deep and agonizing impression. It was a desperate day when the whole nation, wild with joy at the thought of peace, was plunged into inconsolable grief over the death of the great President. It seemed so needless a calamity, and yet it was an event growing out of the very nature of war, out of four years of violence and bloodshed, four years of excited and hysterical thinking. Louisa remembered from her time in Washington how people talked everywhere of how heedless Lincoln was of his own safety, how he avoided his guards whenever it was possible and went unprotected and without fear. She knew also how bitterly and terribly he had been criticized and accused; how people, in the exasperation of disappointment and suffering, let themselves think that everything was the

171

fault of one man, and that man Lincoln. Such accusations, focused at last in one excited brain, grew to the frantic idea that Lincoln was a tyrant and must be made way with. It was the last flaming up of the evil fires of fraternal hate.

Louisa recorded her belief in Lincoln even at a time when almost no one believed in him. She had sympathized so completely with his plans for educating the thousands of slaves to the new duties of freedom and had wanted to share in them. It was heartbreaking for her, and for all who thought as she did, to see those hopes brought utterly to an end.

Throughout the later time of the war and of this sudden sorrow, through her slow gathering of strength so completely broken, she had comforted herself, to a certain degree, by her writing. It was many weeks after her return home before she felt like taking up her pen; but such was the insistence of the demand that, when once she finally did turn herself to her old work, she continued it. After she had completed the papers wanted for the *Commonwealth*, she began to write stories about the war. The interest in the "Hospital Sketches" brought a greater demand for her tales than she found it possible to supply. She commenced a new series of papers in the *Commonwealth* and suddenly stopped in the middle because she felt utterly dissatisfied with them. She realized that she was not doing her best; yet how to find that best she had no idea. She did not know yet that her field of writing was what was real, not what was imaginary. The immediate appreciation of "Hospital Sketches" might have shown her this, but she did not see it. She was puzzled, and being still not well, she was greatly cast down and unhappy.

Two publishers wrote to ask her for the "Hospital Sketches" to be reprinted as a book. One was James Redpath; the other a comparatively new firm, Roberts Brothers. She did not ponder the choice long; she wrote to Roberts Brothers that she preferred another publisher and gave the manuscript to Redpath. Her guardian angel might well have wrung his hands over the decision, but he did not; he seems merely to have contrived that the mistake should not be an irretrievable error. "Hospital Sketches" came out as a book and were read with great interest. They were rapidly and even carelessly written, being for the most part actual letters written during brief intervals of her nursing. Perfection of style was nothing and vividness was everything in the light of her purpose, as she wrote. They were so timely, however, so alive and so full of just what everyone longed to know that they reached an even broader circle of readers than had the *Commonwealth*. She was delighted and surprised, for she thought very little of the sketches herself.

Since the publishers wished for something more, she brought from the cupboard her two novels, over both of which she had toiled fitfully for nearly four years. She showed *Moods* to Redpath and was told that it was too long; so she cast it aside in disappointment and began grinding away at the short stories once more. She tired easily and slept badly, and one night while lying awake she was seized with a plan for shortening and rearranging *Moods* and rose at dawn to begin. In its more abbreviated form it won greater favor with the publishers and was printed by Loring, appearing just before Christmas in 1864.

Louisa finally came to speak of the poor book as "a picked robin," seeing later that she had not improved it by her frequent changes. She liked always to remember that Henry James, Senior, spoke of it with commendation, and that he and Mrs. James came to see her while she was staying in Boston for a brief visit. They asked her to dinner and she enjoyed going. She spoke with a smile afterward of the grave advice given her by Henry James, Junior, then a very young "literary youth," as she called him. Her short, curly hair made her look very immature and boyish, whereas she really felt immeasurably older than the grave Henry, who was just at the threshold of his own extraordinarily brilliant career. *Moods* was well received for a time but it did not have a very long life. People who had read "Hospital Sketches" wanted something rather different from Miss Alcott who could write so truthfully and vividly about the war, a subject which in the hands of many brought forth only romancing and lies.

As the immediate success of *Moods* passed Louisa lost heart completely. She remarked finally that she was tired of long stories, that she would rather "fall back on rubbishy tales, for they pay best and I can't starve on praise." It was a belief unworthy of her, unworthy of her real powers, of her father's principles, of Emerson's teaching. It was, however, almost the inevitable state of mind of a person who has struggled bravely through months of illness, has tried to work in spite of bodily weakness, but who feels at last that nothing will ever be better.

Things, just the same, were bound to be better for one of Louisa's spirit. She was a strange mixture of impetuousness and toiling perseverance, of wild, impossible fancies and practical sense. It was these steadier qualities which kept her struggling forward during those dreary months when health seemed impossibly far away. Time, however, the great element in such illness as hers, did finally do its work. The summer after the appearance of *Moods*, the summer after peace came, she was really better at last. She could see the world suddenly with clearer and more reasonable eyes; she sighed less for the unattainable plans she had made for serving her country further and began to take firmer hold of her real occupation.

It was very stimulating to have two and finally three companies and various magazines asking her for work, when once everything that she could write had begged its way from one publishing door to another. She still could not work for very long hours at a stretch; but she sat in the Orchard House garden, on the bench which her father had built about the great elm, and fell to dreaming once more vigorous, constructive dreams of the former Louisa variety. Like all people when they are ill, she had been thinking only of the difficult present and not of the future. Now as she began to feel something like real strength again she fell to wondering what was before her. She had thought of herself as such a failure, but perhaps after all there were still worlds for her to conquer.

# CHAPTER EIGHT

*❧ ❧ ❧*

# Laurie

RECOVERY FROM LONG ILLNESS OFTEN SEEMS like beginning life all over again. When, for months, strength has seemed to be gone forever, its return appears to make all sorts of impossible thing possible, and to show life spreading out in new and alluring prospects. It might have been thought that Louisa's hospital experience, which ended in such disaster, would have quenched some of her love of adventure and of seeking after new things. Such was not the case at all. The moment she began to feel like her old self again she wanted to see more and to do more than she had ever dreamed of before.

The journey to Washington was the longest which she had ever taken and was the first which seemed to show her a really new portion of the world. She had seen only a small, infinitely troubled bit of it, to be sure, on that adventure, but she had been in that part of it which bordered upon tremendous affairs. Concord seemed rather limited, seemed very sheltered and remote to her, after all that she had seen and taken part in during her time in Washington. In her very early years she had so little opportunity for travel that it was only now that she discovered how fully she had inherited her father's love of wandering.

The interval of her nursing and her illness had cut through all of her old habits of living, had brought to an end what former engagements she had for teaching and sewing. After the months of confinement through sickness and recovery she longed with a great desire to do something entirely different, to see unknown things and to build up some new memories which would do away with those unhappy recollections of suffering and delirium which still would haunt her mind.

For the first time she was earning enough from her writing to be able to dignify the returns by the name of income. Whatever she received she spent immediately upon her family; since it gave her unbounded pleasure to be able at last to pay debts, to buy comforts, and to see her mother's anxious face relaxing a little under the peaceful knowledge of growing security. If Louisa were to travel, as she more and more desired to do, she must find some means for making her way as she went. Such was not an easy prospect for a person whose health was not yet completely what it had once been and who had no experience of going about the world. She was obliged to wait and, being Louisa, waited rather impatiently for the opportunity to carry out her wish.

Under the spur of ever-present restlessness she worked fitfully but intensely upon her stories and the much-tried novel, *Success*, in which Theodore Parker appeared under an altered name. Perhaps in memory of what he had said of her she had given the book its title. She still wrote war stories; but finally flung one down in disgust, announcing that it was "flat, patriotic and done to order." She was wondering somewhat discontentedly what she would attack next when the chance for which she had dreamed and longed, the possibility of a journey abroad, finally presented itself.

A friend of the Alcott family had an invalid daughter who wished to travel in Europe but who was not well enough to go alone. It was suggested that perhaps Louisa would go with her as nurse and companion. Louisa did not stop to reflect very long. If she had, she would perhaps have realized that the duties which went with this offer were not like those of regular nursing and might be hard and wearing upon her kind of person. She consented and made ready inside of a week.

It was in the middle of July that the steamer *China* sailed from Boston, bearing the invalid friend and Louisa. Truly she felt that the world and all its highways were before her when she saw the blue Atlantic rolling away to the horizon. She could hardly believe that presently she was to see a foreign shore rise up on that eastward edge of the earth which all of her life had seemed to her only an unbroken line of infinite distance.

They landed in England and stayed long enough for a mere glimpse of London. To anyone of Louisa's ideas London meant hardly more than one thing, Dickens. She could have spent weeks there; for the dark, drizzly city was the goal of her most cherished desire. But there was too little time; presently they crossed to Belgium, saw a small portion of France and embarked on a leisurely boat journey up the Rhine.

She never tried to tell anyone just what her romantic soul felt during those days of winding travel up the valley of the famous river, with its mountains crowned with woods, with the steep-roofed villages coming down to the water's edge, and with each little town dominated by its tall-spired church and its castle on the hill above. What did she think when for the first time she stood looking at a real castle, battlemented and turreted, along whose walls Roderigo might have

180

walked with his noble stride? She smiled a little to remember how familiarly she had once written tales of castles and countesses, when she had so little conception of what both really were. It is to be noted that after seeing the reality she she never wrote of those extravagant fancies again.

She stopped at Frankfort to see the house of Goethe; for Louisa would never be anything but an ardent hero-worshipper and here was the shrine of one of her literary idols. Then there was further travel to the southward, with the Alps coming into view, a far, white dream of mountains, impossibly high. At Vevey they ceased their incessant moving about, since for the sake of the friend's health, they were to spend some time in Switzerland.

Late October saw them safely established at the Pension Victoria, glad to be done for the moment with wandering. The proprietress was an English woman who knew how to make her guests comfortable and who took pride in the welfare of her transient household. We can have no doubt that Louisa's good spirits and friendliness soon won the two Americans as many pleasant acquaintances as they desired. Only one party of guests stood out against her, a Southern colonel and his family, who regarded her across the room with the bitter enmity which is the aftermath of war. Louisa smiled over their haughty hostility and cheerfully went her own way.

Some pleasant Scottish sisters were staying there also. They had known Walter Scott and could tell Louisa of him. She enjoyed them, and the English people who came and went and were so good-mannered and friendly. It was such things which Louisa loved to get out of travel, knowledge of her fellow men, absorbing talk with them of all that they had heard and seen, of the interesting people whom they knew, in turn. In spite, however, of the good care and pleasant company, Louisa now had leisure to face and to admit an unhappy truth, the fact that, so far as she was concerned, the expedition was really proving a failure.

It was evident that she was not suited by nature to the exacting task which she had undertaken. She was unselfish and considerate always and never grudged her service to ailing people. But she was not entirely well herself, was still nervous and impatient, and she was, moreover, possessed of a thousand times more interest and enthusiasm than was her companion. It was very hard for her to be hampered by the inabilities of another. Often she was kept from seeing what she wished and from learning what she longed to know by the lack of strength and the disinclination of one whose wishes were so different from her own. She was beginning to be troubled and unbelievably disappointed; she had fallen into rather low spirits when the most interesting and illuminating incident of the whole journey suddenly came to pass.

The big diligence came jingling into Vevey, the conveyance that was like a huge carriage, three times the ordinary size, boasting a postilion with a horn and drawn by four horses with bells on their harness. From this romantic vehicle there was put down a new member for the household of the Pension Victoria. This was a young man, a very young man not more than eighteen or twenty years old, a Polish lad with a thin, white face, black hair, and excitable dark eyes. His charming manners were evident from the first moment wherein he was introduced to all the residents of the pension, among them to "Mademoiselle Alcott from America." He was called, so the mistress of ceremonies explained with some difficulty, Ladislas Wisniewski.

"He is sick," Louisa pronounced to herself on her first glance at the pale, bright-eyed boy. She saw him shivering in a chilly draught and straightway arranged to have his seat at the table changed to one nearer the great, warm porcelain stove. He voiced his gratitude in broken English and was her slave from that moment.

Although he proved to be twelve years younger than Louisa, it was hard for anyone to speak of him truthfully as a boy. The experiences behind him seemed to make that impossible. He was a student in a Polish university when a revolution broke out in his country and he, with some college friends, was among the first to take up arms against the Russian sovereignty over their country. The outbreak was not successful and led to his being imprisoned for many months. When he was finally set free, he was ill and was threatened with very serious complications of the lungs. He was poor and friendless and he was banished from his own country. He had come to Switzerland in the hope of restoring his health, broken down by those ruthless months in a damp, airless, military dungeon. He still wore the blue and white uniform of the Polish Revolutionists. He and cordial, sympathetic Louisa immediately became fast friends.

Louisa Alcott had lovers during her varied life; that much we know. She even tells us of one whom she acquired at the age of fifteen and of how she suddenly saw that he was sentimental and silly and lost her enthusiasm for him with great abruptness. She has been less frank about the others, so that who they were and just what she thought of them are secrets of her own which prying eyes have no right to investigate, not even in the name of her cherished fame.

It is said that at the time Anna was engaged
Louisa had an ardent suitor who urged marriage
upon her. She had no feeling for him at all, but
asked her mother whether she ought not to
accept him for the sake of mending the family
fortunes. Wise Abba Alcott persuaded her
daughter out of any such romantic fancy of
self-sacrifice; for what could be a more pathetic
sight than independent, impatient Louisa married to a person for whom she did not care? She
spoke later with much irreverent jesting of an
admirer who observed her on the train, followed
her home, and hung languishing about the
house, writing letters and sending flowers to his
inaccessible adored one. Great was the mirth of
all the girls over this episode, to which Louisa,
speaking of the affair in her journal, added the
postscript that her lovers always seemed to be
absurd.

What is nearer the truth is that Louisa always
treated them so lightly that they appeared ridiculous. She was so busy, so absorbed in her family
and in what she hoped to do for them, that she
rarely gave thought to matrimony. There have
been several elderly gentlemen who have con-
fessed in their late years to having cherished in
youth a tender feeling for Louisa Alcott. Did she
ever see it, one wonders, or seeing it, take any
note of it whatsoever? It is hard to be sure. Life
was so full for her without marriage, so beset

with activities and responsibilities, that certainly matrimony was something which she never consciously missed. She had a great desire for independence, which it would have been hard for her to give up for any person's sake. On the other hand she had great capacity for affection and sentiment, for romance and for happiness. Did she ever bestow that affection upon any congenial person of her own age, the sort of affection which she poured out upon Mr. Emerson and Theodore Parker? We do not know.

This friendship with Ladislas, ardent as it was, could never be called a love affair. It is one of those cheerful, genuine things which after all these years can still warm us with the knowledge of the happiness which it brought. Louisa had lived always in reticent New England where people do not speak much of their feelings or make any show of them. Ladislas was a revelation to her in his immediate frank admiration and later, in his openhearted devotion.

They had delightful days together and a world of small adventures. He taught her French and she instructed him in English. They rowed on the lake, they explored the grounds of the chateau, they took tramps along the mountainsides, and looked down upon the fair landscape below. They talked incessantly. In the evenings Ladislas would play in the pension parlor, for he was a finished musician, with a depth of feeling in his art which met Louisa's sensitive perception in her own. Everyone liked him, petted him on account of his ill health, enjoyed his attractive charm. For two months the pleasant intercourse went on, with the snow-capped mountains and the broad blue lake for a background.

There is romance in friendship as well as in actual love. It was here for Louisa, a romance of the friendly sort, which enlarged her education and opened her eyes to a thousand things which she had not known before. Approval and devotion were extraordinarily good for her. Shy and distrustful of her own powers, conscious all her life of a certain tall awkwardness, she had never really had sufficient confidence in herself, she had never understood in the least that her gay spirits and enlivening company made up a hundred times over for any lack of gentle charm. Few people had ever been allowed to come close enough to her to tell her what she really was. Now, without need for words, the openly adoring companionship of Ladislas told her that she was unusual and delightful.

She got much also from his clever talk which he carried on with such confiding frankness. She looked more deeply than she ever could have done before into the heart and mind of an eager, intelligent young man. She learned a tremendous amount from him about Switzerland, about people, and especially about his particular kind of a person. Of all their times together she remembered longest the mild, windy November morning of her birthday when they walked together, half in sunshine and half in shade, through the stately chateau garden and looked out on the changing, glorious colors of the lake. A few more happy weeks went by, then the time inevitably came when the plan of travel carried Louisa forward with her invalid friend into Italy.

The two were to spend the rest of the winter in Nice. Louisa liked the bold mountain country better than the charm of sleepy blue waters and the wreaths of flowers everywhere. Her discontent with her work became greater and greater now that she had not the diversion of a devoted friend to help the time pass. She thought a great deal about Ladislas; she thought even more about her family at home. When she was near those dear ones, she was so occupied in caring for them that she did not see each one as he or she actually was. Now she pictured them constantly in her heart and seemed to know and understand them better than she ever had before. She could see fully what was the beauty and courage of Elizabeth's short life. Even from this great distance she could watch how Anna was fulfilling the promise of earlier years, how her industry and devotion were illuminating the lives of her husband and two little sons; for a second boy had very recently arrived. Louisa could grieve over the obvious weariness and feebleness which were so visibly creeping over her mother; she could rejoice that her father's long years of deep thinking and study were at last beginning to be crowned with honors. Why had she not realized all that so clearly when she was at home?

It began to be plain to her that "little May," the baby of the family, had grown into a brilliant and ambitious young woman with hopes and aspirations very much like Louisa's own. These two were alike in temperament in various ways, so much alike that in their earlier years they had often clashed. The gentleness which dwelt in Anna and Elizabeth was quite absent in these two militant spirits. Even as she skirmished with her, Louisa loved and admired her younger sister. She toiled for her, planned for her, sewed for her by the hour. It was Louisa's greatest pride that the first ball dress which she ever tried to make was a glorious success and that May looked like a princess in it. We do not hear of Louisa's ever having made a ball dress for herself. A most ambitious seamstress was Louisa, for she did not stop at ball dresses; she even made riding habits, and somehow got means that would produce the horses upon which to ride. It was such a delight to her to see May get what she wanted.

Now, in the midst of all the stimulating beauty about her, in ancient flower-decked Italy, Louisa thought more and more of her younger sister and of how May would get so much out of all this richness of beauty which was all about her. The old differences were quite forgotten. Once these two reached an age sufficient for understanding each other, the little-girl quarrels ceased forever. May must not have as hard a time as she had known, Louisa determined; she must have training and encouragement; she should have beauty about her and an abundant life, with everything to fill it to the brim with happiness, comfort, opportunity, lovers. It seems that a final idea must have slipped through Louisa's mind, the thought that, though Ladislas was far too young to be anything but a friend for her, he could be, in the realms of romantic fancy, an ardent and appropriate lover for May.

Louisa saw the carnival at Nice and the magnificent Easter ceremonies. She attended some glorious performances of Italian tragic acting. Then suddenly on a sunny spring day, with the scent of roses everywhere in the air, she arose with a firm determination in her heart to go home. She had spent all the time and care upon her ailing companion which she had promised, and she knew that now there were others at hand to take her place. Spring was beautiful in Italy, but the disappearing snow wreaths in New England, the faint green which would be beginning to cloud the tall elms, the beloved family which seemed so desperately far away — she must and would see them all. She longed, moreover, for her freedom, for that independence of mind and body which were part of her very being. She laid the matter before her friend, formulated plans, and was very soon away upon her homeward journey. How happy, how wonderfully happy she was to be free!

She was to stop first in Paris and then in England, so that she might see something more of those famous places around which her interest and fancy were chiefly centered. As the train roared into the station she was astounded to see Ladislas, waving his blue and white cap to her over the heads of the crowd. She knew that he was in Paris, but she had no notion of how he could have divined when she was to arrive. That, he explained later, was quite simple. He had heard her say vaguely that she might come to Paris and he knew that in such a case she would lodge at Madame Dync's. By going nearly every day and inquiring whether Madame Dyne had any news he at last found out just when Louisa was coming. He was now entirely at her service and wished to put the whole of his knowledge at her disposal so that she might see the most possible in her short two weeks.

Somewhere in an indefinite region beyond the river he and his two other Polish revolutionary friends were living in the barest and narrowest of poverty. Ladislas was trying to earn money by translating. He had known little English until Louisa began to teach him; now he felt himself so proficient that he was putting *Vanity Fair* into Polish. He was having some difficulty with certain terms of English slang and brought Louisa lists of impossible passages for her to make clear to him. She helped him with all her heart, while he, in turn, introduced her to the beauties of Paris.

The great city was a brilliant and glittering place just then, under the spectacular rule of the Emperor Napoleon III. After several experiments in government, the republic had drifted into allowing him to become Emperor of the French, with autocratic power in his hands — for as long as he could hold it. He and his beautiful Empress had the definite policy that show and pomp and parade were the foundation of imperial strength, and by such means he was trying to steady an already uncertain throne. Napoleon and Eugenie were deliberately striving to outdo in extravagance of display all the other courts of Europe. It may not have been wise, but it made a magnificent pageant for travelers from afar. The processions, the illuminations, the gorgeous festivals in the gardens and in the old palaces, as well as the picture galleries and the ancient churches, all these were there for Louisa to see in the whirlwind panorama of two exciting weeks. It was hard to part with Ladislas at the end of the brief time. It seems quite certain what Louisa felt about him. What he felt is not quite so plain.

"I shall never see you again," he cried at the last minute, in Polish abandon, as he kissed her hand. His hollow cheeks and his pathetic cough made her own heart sink with misgiving for him. She bade him good-bye courageously; but it was hard to go.

Her stay in England was as gay and delightful as had been the visit in Paris. Introductions through publishers opened various pleasant doors to her, so that she was invited here and there, in London and in the country. She loved nothing so much in all of this period of her travels as the thatched farmhouses, the fields yellow with gorse, the skylarks, and the blossoming hawthorne. She met a great many of the distinguished people of the day; she saw Dickens and heard him read. It was possible for her to arrange with an English publisher to bring out *Moods* and she was asked for another book. Everywhere she was made much of as Miss Alcott, the American authoress. She began to feel like somebody, instead of being just drudging Louisa, nurse and companion. It is good for modest people to feel like somebody now and then.

None of this pleasure, however, made her delay an hour on the real journey upon which she was bound. In July she sailed from Liverpool, and after a long and stormy voyage got home just a year after her departure. She burst into the house. Nowhere all along the way had there been such joy for her as there was in this homecoming.

It seemed as though she looked at them with new eyes, after having been so long away. Her mother seemed much older and had evidently had no easy time without the strong support of Louisa. Anna looked hard-worked; happy May was bursting with plans; the two Pratt babies were deliciously plump and affectionate. Louisa discovered that her mother had been obliged to borrow funds to keep the family afloat while she was having the last weeks of freedom in France and England. It was plain that Louisa had done well to worry about them and to speed home to take care of them. Her effects were not even unpacked before she had herself at work to meet their uncomplaining needs.

There enters now upon the scene the real good fairy of Louisa's fortunes. Other things she had gained through relentless striving. But this great event of her life came about by what some people might call luck, but others would know was a well-deserved blessing of Providence. Louisa was at last to find what had been so long awaiting her.

Mr. Thomas Niles, partner and manager of the publishing company of Roberts Brothers, had surveyed Louisa from afar, watching her career and reading what she had written. He shook his head over the melodramatic tales; he looked through her novel *Moods*, well-spoken of for a little time, but bringing no final success. His kindly dark eyes brightened when he read the *Hospital Sketches*, and as has been said, he wrote to her proposing that when the articles were made into a book, his company should bring them out. To Louisa he was merely a name, as someone whom her father knew, who had to do with books. When she declined his offer, Mr. Niles said nothing, but waited.

As Louisa began writing again after her travels, this interested and far-seeing personage appeared upon the scene once more. He was a dark, spare, slow-spoken man of discerning tastes. People talked of him as "a confirmed bachelor," who lived with some cousins on Beacon Street in winter and in a beautiful old house in Arlington in the summer. Although he had no family of his own he had so strong an element of fairy godmother in his nature that he was in close accord with all the youthful persons in any way connected with him. Since he was one of fifteen children his kindred were rather many. He had these young readers in mind when he made a suggestion to Louisa.

"I think, Miss Alcott," he told her, "that you could write a book for girls. I should like to see you try."

Louisa replied both to him and to herself that she knew nothing about girls, that she liked and understood boys better, and that she had no appropriate ideas to put into such a story. She was too busy just then or thought that she was, to consider the plan seriously. She went to Boston in the early winter after her mother had recovered from a serious illness. Louisa took a high-up room in Hayward Place and wrote industriously. Money began to come in for the family necessities, but not in a very copious stream. She was beginning to feel hard pressed for funds when finally Mr. Niles, mild, patient, and wise, said gently and again:

"I think, Miss Alcott, that you should write a story for girls."

This time she heeded the advice. She was so desperate that she was ready to attempt anything. Some people are stimulated by one thing, some by another. With Louisa, it was to be the spur of poverty which brought her to her most important venture. She began.

She had gone home in February to be with her mother, who was still not well. It was in May of the year 1868 that she actually took up the new enterprise.

"I don't know anything about girls, except just ourselves," she lamented dejectedly to her mother. Several times in earlier years the idea had flitted through her mind that she might make a story of her own family and their varied trials and struggles. The plan came back to her now. Yes, it might do. At least she would try it.

The undertaking did not seem so impossible once she had set out upon it. Without her intending it, all the scenes which she described seemed to center about the brown hillside house where they had begun to live when she was thirteen and where she had spent her happiest years. The games on the hill, the plays in the barn, the work, the small differences, all the ups and downs of their family life began to take their appointed places in the story. Louisa's fine, intrepid mother entered into the narrative, just as

197

she had entered into everything else that any of her girls had done. The beautiful story of *Pilgrim's Progress*, which was the favorite of their early reading, interwove itself with many of the chapters as they developed. Of her father, Louisa did not seem able to say so much as of her mother. He was so unlike usual men that she felt herself not quite equal to the task of showing him to others, particularly to young readers, in all his true dignity and worth. Yet the beauty of his ideas slipped in somehow and gave the work a different aspect from that of any ordinary tale.

Every book, even though it has four heroines, must also have a hero. There was a dear friend of the Alcott family, Alfred Whitman, a yellow-haired, cheery, friendly boy who had lived for some time in Anna's house after she was married so that he might go to Mr. Sanborn's school in Concord. Many of his small adventures with the girls came into the story. But as far as personality went it was not Alfred Whitman who presently began to take definite place in what Louisa was writing. A black-haired lad, full of music and gaiety, of adventurous good spirits which matched Louisa's own, pathetic in his loneliness at first, a matchless friend when once he entered into the family affections, such was Laurie. It was probable that not even Louisa realized at first that he was

Ladislas Wisnicwski come to life upon the page. She was warming to her task now as the story marched forward.

All her old misgivings came back, however, when she saw the first dozen chapters lying ready to be submitted to the hopeful Mr. Niles. There was nothing exciting or adventurous in them, she thought, only the commonplace narration of everyday affairs. She had been sure all along that she could not write for girls. And yet — no person of genius ever does his or her best without knowing it. Louisa knew in her heart that it was good.

Since her advisor was anxious to see even the beginning of the story, she mailed the first chapters at once to Mr. Niles. We can picture him as carrying the package home to reread in the quiet of his own library overlooking the Charles River. He read while the lights pricked out upon the bridges and along the banks in the late-coming June darkness. He finally laid down the manuscript with a sigh. It was not somehow just what he had imagined it was going to be. A kindly, gray-haired bachelor is not always the best judge of a book for growing girls.

Being honest, he wrote frankly to Louisa. He had some doubts, he told her, about the success of the book but he was anxious to see the remainder.

Anyone except Louisa would have given up the attempt at that point. But she had begun to see her work in its proper light; she understood also that just such stories were needed for young readers instead of the sentimental and tragic tales with which their minds were usually fed. She went boldly forward in spite of Mr. Niles' letter.

Somewhat earlier, Mr. Niles had written to ask her what was to be the name of the book. That she was able to answer immediately. He knitted his brows a little over her rapid backhand writing as he read. She called it, she said, *Little Women.*

# CHAPTER NINE

## "Little Women"

To one who has gone through all of her life in the ordinary sunshine and shade of bright hopes and unavoidable disappointments, it is very strange to stand all at once in the artificial spotlight of totally unexpected fame. From the moment her book appeared, life was entirely changed for unassuming Louisa Alcott. She simply did not know what to make of it when letters began to come pouring in, when visitors arrived in numbers scarcely less extravagant, when people pursued her everywhere to get an autograph, a word, or even nothing but a good stare at the renowned Miss Alcott, author of the new success, *Little Women*.

She had finished the book bravely, ending with Meg's engagement, since she felt that young readers would not care to go forward into the more romantic period of her heroines' lives. It was with some trepidation that she sent the whole to Mr. Niles, for he had been so obviously disappointed over the first chapters. He was equally frank now. He did not find the story as absorbing as he had hoped; it might be better after all to give up the idea of publishing it. But first, he would lay it before some young friends of his, girls of just the age for which it was written, to find what was their opinion.

Oh wise Thomas Niles, to understand that his bachelor judgment was not final in the matter and to take into consultation the only real experts, the young ladies themselves. The first to see the manuscript was his niece, Lily Almy, who lived at Longwood. She galloped through it and rendered a verdict so breathless with enthusiasm that her uncle paused and thought again. He showed it to another girl and another. Every one of them spoke of it in just the same way; they all of them loved it.

It is hard to think of *Little Women* as read for the first time; it is to us a tale so hallowed by the association of our mother's and our grandmother's delight in it, before our own day. A completely fresh story it was to them, a book even of a kind different from anything they had read before, a book just about themselves, so it seemed, by someone who understood them completely. It is no wonder that the first readers were enchanted with it. It is to the wisdom and appreciation of those young people that we owe the fact that *Little Women* was not hidden away forever in that spidery cupboard where Louisa's early failures were tossed in despair. We thank them from our hearts, and Mr. Niles for listening to them.

He heard their raptures with some astonishment and read the manuscript through again. On the strength of their delight in it he decided to bring it out. We all know what followed. It was almost the first book of its kind, a direct, natural, truthful tale, with no straining after emotion and effect. It was just what girls had been starving for, although scarcely anyone knew it. Louisa did, when she refused to give up, even in the face of Thomas Niles' disappointment. He cannot be blamed for not seeing the value of the story immediately. Without his wisdom in suggesting it, in persevering with the suggestion, and in leaving the final decision to the girls themselves, there would have been no *Little Women*. There would have been only a splendid idea in the brain of a busy author who never found time to reduce it to writing or to print.

Louisa put into it everything out of her own life and those of her sisters. It was in the shabby brown house, Hillside, with its garden and fruit trees and barn that the most happy and most truly childlike of her years had been spent. The house in *Little Women*, however, sounds somewhat more like the Orchard House where the Alcotts were living when Louisa wrote the story. Hillside is more evidently Plumfield, the scene of *Little Men*. The name March rather naturally follows from the suggestion of the name May, a somewhat mild surname for that storm-tossed Abba, who lived through so many ups and downs. The Brook Farm connection with the Pratt family made John Pratt receive the name of John Brooke. He appears in one or two other stories and always the same; for his steady sincerity and goodness follow the lines of an exact portrait. Anna's contented happiness gave Louisa her knowledge, shown here and elsewhere, of what unmeasured beauty there can be in married life. Louisa put Elizabeth into the story bodily, with all her gentleness and unflinching courage. She showed May to the life, a little spoiled by the others' petting, a person of great charm and the recipient of many happy gifts, as Louisa was the dispenser of them.

The real power of the book, however, centers about Jo. She was Louisa to the life, more so, perhaps, than the author ever dreamed of making her. Louisa's honest opinion of herself was so very humble that she made not the slightest effort to dress up her counterpart in the semblance of a conventional heroine. Her picture of Jo is the farthest thing removed from flattery.

She has told frankly of every drawback in her appearance and her nature, her round shoulders, her long-limbed awkwardness, her thorny moods, her headlong mistakes, her quick flashes of temper. Yet Jo is lovable beyond words and more real than any of the others. She is real because Louisa understood her even better than the rest; she stands out from the background because Louisa herself was such a magnificent character that a truthful study of her becomes, without any intention, a splendid figure also.

Louisa's kind but outwardly severe grandfather, known only during the Temple School period of their life in Boston, was put into the book as Mr. Lawrence, the grandfather of Laurie. She has declared that "Aunt March is no one," but her family say otherwise. They all see in that autocratically generous lady the reflection of no other than the great Aunt Hancock, with her connections in high places, her family tyranny, and her good heart. Louisa could not remember her; but the family legend was enough, and Aunt Hancock lives on in thoroughly Aunt Hancock-ish fashion. In some of the kind relatives who were so kind to Jo and Amy we surely see good Cousin Lizzie Wells. Not all of the minor figures can be traced to their originals; but it is safe to say that they all lived and that Louisa knew them.

With *Little Women*, Louisa achieved what she really wanted, a piece of work which she actually knew to be her best. With it she achieved also the appreciation of the world and such prosperity as gave her full power at last to do just what she wished. It is delightful to read of how her name came to be on every tongue; how she grew to be not merely famous, which mattered little to her, but universally beloved, which mattered much. After all the years of doubting her own powers, of looking for her true field, of thinking of herself as a struggling failure, she was obliged at last to admit, even in the depths of her own soul, that she was a success.

It is a joy also to know of what she did with the generous prosperity which came to her so suddenly. After a whole lifetime of poverty she felt as though the magic purse of Fortunatus was thrust all at once into her hands. The Alcott family now moved no more. Louisa had said when they took up their abode in the Orchard House that she hoped they would not stir again for twenty years. It was owing to her that they did not. She could at last make the place comfortable, the dilapidated old building which the last owner had thought fit only for firewood.

Here, in the big bedroom where the sun came flooding in, Abba Alcott, feeble now, and no longer toiling and busy, could sit all day with her knitting and sewing and the beloved books which for so many years there had been so little time to read. How often Louisa had said that she wanted a *sunny* room for her mother, pathetic record of the dark and cheerless lodgings into which their narrow means had frequently brought them! Her father's study was equipped with extra bookcases to hold his cherished library and the long shelves of his journals, bound by Louisa's order, so that they could be safe for generations to come. There are some tremendous ideas embodied in those journals, chiefly about education; for Bronson had theories so far in advance of his time that even in our day we have not caught up with all of them, although we have accepted many. It used to be thought, and not so long ago, that the windows of a schoolroom must have white paint on all the lower panes, to keep the children from looking out, and incidentally to keep light and sunshine from coming in. It was Bronson Alcott who first opened the windows of schoolrooms to more than one kind of sunshine and who has made learning brighter for all time.

It was a great and glorious day when Louisa had a furnace put into the Orchard House, so that the picturesque open fires need no longer be the sole source of heat. Not so very many years earlier, she had, one day, a dreadful battle with herself, wanting to spend a carefully saved sum of money on tickets to a concert, when all the while the chilly feet of her beloved family marched back and forth on cold matting in a room whose draughty floor cried aloud for a carpet. She resisted the temptation and bought the rug; but now at last she could do more than make a cold house a little less cold; she could make it actually warm and cheery. She thought of everything, from flannel petticoats upward, to make her beloved ones safe, comfortable and happy in every spiritual and practical way possible.

Amongst all these matters, she thought of not one single thing to do for herself. Her own room in the house is plain and small and modestly furnished, standing today just as it did in her own time. On the table lies the shabby black leather writing case, in which she wrote upon her knee, for she had no desk. She had begun her career of authorship on a little table in the tiny room off the Hillside garden; she had continued it in sky parlors and odd corners of casual lodgings with so few conveniences for writers that she never missed them now. All of her life she had dreamed of what she would get for her family and had never found time for plans concerning what she might get for herself.

Meanwhile, Mr. Thomas Niles, walking with his dogs along the bank of Mystic Pond, sitting in the garden of the pleasant old Arlington house, was hatching other plans. A clever publisher was Thomas Niles, one of the most brilliant and enterprising of his time. He was watching the growing popularity of *Little Women* and presently had a new suggestion to make to Miss Alcott. The book must have a sequel.

She made almost as much demur as she had the first time. She was writing about children; no one would be interested in seeing the girls married. After long persuasion, after being shown multitudes of letters always making one and the same request, she gave in. She made one reservation, however, even as she agreed.

"I won't marry Jo to Laurie to please anybody."

The first part of *Little Women* was published in October of the year 1868. Mr. Niles offered Louisa a certain sum for the copyright of the book, which seemed very large indeed to her unaccustomed eyes. He urged her, however, to make a different arrangement under which she would receive a royalty so long as the book was sold. It was his principle that publishing was best carried on by being as fair and as generous with the authors as it was possible to be. It is a happy record, that of his connection with Louisa Alcott. His company never had a greater success than the two achieved with *Little Women.*

He found and brought out the work of many another person who was to become famous: Jean Ingelow, Emily Dickinson, Thomas Bailey Aldrich, Susan Coolidge, Helen Hunt Jackson, Edward Everett Hale, and numberless others. Great writers of the day were his intimate friends in spite of his odd, slow-spoken ways. It is told that Thomas Bailey Aldrich and William Dean Howells would often come into his office to see him, but would be found by others, arriving later, to be reading the morning papers, since Thomas Niles seemed to have so little to say to them. They so enjoyed the presence of this charming silent man that they were quite content with a visit even if it lacked conversation. He was very conservative in spite of all his enterprise in undertaking new ventures. It is told of him that when telephones came into use he would never talk into one, but always had the message given and received through another person. The last of those three cousins with whom he lived says that they knew all the authors of their day, that most of them came to the house, but that none were as delightful to have there as Louisa Alcott, who was always overflowing with good spirits and good talk, the very best company in the world.

With Thomas Niles she formed one of those valuable friendships which were milestones in her life. He was her counselor in all literary matters, a willing and devoted guide through the rest of her career. Financial affairs were never to be difficult for her again, with such a source of income and with such good advice as to what to do with it. He began by being a friend of Bronson Alcott's — he was to end by being Louisa's literary mentor and by making her fortune.

It was no wonder, therefore, that Louisa finally heeded his urging to write a sequel to *Little Women*, to be brought out in the spring. She set herself to work in November and finished very quickly, sending him the manuscript on New Year's Day. It carried the story of the girls forward into the beginning of being grown up, into living "with their own wings," as the Dutch translator has put it. It showed Anna's wedding, with the guests dancing under the Revolutionary elm. It brought to a briefly worded end the simple tragedy of Elizabeth's short life, the Beth whom every reader has mourned, not merely because of what Louisa said of her, but because of what she was.

Since neither Louisa nor May were married, it was necessary to expand into the realm of the imagination to supply the desired conclusion for the book. Amy was taken abroad, to see all those glorious things which Louisa wanted so much to have May see, when she herself first had the opportunity for travel. At Vevey, where Louisa met Ladislas, Amy was described as meeting Laurie again and floating on the lake, these two imaginary ones pledged their lives to each other. And as for Jo, she was dutifully provided with a husband, but what an unexpected one!

Where, everyone has wondered for all these years, where did Louisa find the model for Professor Bhaer? Is he the ideal combination of qualities which she thought might possibly have touched her own heart? It may be. There is a little of her father in that good Mr. Bhaer, a very little; there is a trace of Mr. Emerson in his high principles and his advice to wayward Jo. There is also something of Louisa's more distantly idealized hero, Goethe, in his Germanic make-up. No record of her own, nor any memory of her surviving family, gives evidence of there having been a real person to stand for that portrait. He is somehow less convincing than any of her other characters. This is not surprising, since even in her own mind a satisfactory lover for the counterpart of Louisa Alcott did not exist.

In the rather shadowy figure of the March girls' father, it is hard to recognize Bronson Alcott. Louisa always meant to write a book which should have her father as the central character; she spoke of it by various names, *The*

*Cost of an Idea* or *An Old-Fashioned Boy*. She had thought of it and spoken of it long before she undertook *Little Women*. She was so unlike Bronson that, although she was devoted to him, there were certain of his ideas which she did not truly comprehend, certain phases of his life to which she felt that she could not do justice, since she did not quite fathom the motives which lay behind them. She waited all of her life for the moment when she really would understand him fully; and she waited too long, for the book was never written. Perhaps it was because she had this plan still in view that she did not make a more striking figure out of the father of Meg, Jo, Beth, and Amy. But in one matter we see her true affection for him coming into the very center of the stage.

In almost the last chapter of *Little Women*, when Jo is married and the whole family sits about discussing plans for the future, Jo broaches her great idea of what is to be done with Plumfield, the "beautiful old place" in the country left her by Aunt March. She announces that she and Professor Bhaer are going to have a school there. She describes the school — it is to be for boys, for rich boys whose parents neglect them and leave them to servants, so that they have no chance for proper growing up, and for poor boys who would never have proper

opportunities to learn. They are to be taught —
but there is no use in going into the details of
the plan. It is, briefly, the school of which Bronson Alcott always dreamed, the perfect school
which he — so nearly — knew how to put into
being. The actual realization of it came as close
to existing as it ever managed to in that idea
sponsored by a public-spirited man for the public
schools of Germantown, in which Bronson and
Abba Alcott took such happy and such brief part
during the first unclouded years of their married
life. What was it that Jo said of the plan in
*Little Women*? Her husband could "teach and
train the boys in his own way," while she could
keep house for them all and "feed and pet and
scold them" to her heart's content. Out of the
vanished years comes, in that brief passage, the
vision of that glorious dream in Germantown;
out of the past comes the figure of Reuben
Haines with his high-collared gray Quaker coat
and his deep, far-seeing eyes. He and the Alcotts
had to do with the founding of two schools. One
is the Germantown Academy, child of Reuben
Haines' first plan and still educating children as
he hoped to educate them. That, however, is not
the only school which he had a share in estab-
lishing. The other is Plumfield.

The second part of *Little Women* was received with as much acclaim as the first, so that

Thomas Niles immediately applied to Louisa for another book to be issued the following year. He may have been a little worried for fear, since Louisa had apparently completed the record of her own family, she might not be able to go on as successfully as she had begun. She did not need the Marches, however; but launched out into a new tale, *An Old-Fashioned Girl*.

The heroine of this, Polly, is not Louisa herself, but the adventures and trials through which Polly went follow very closely her own tribulations in her early effort to make a living. Louisa at the time said very little of the difficulties, the disappointments, and the slights which made those years such hard ones to a person of her sensitive, hopeful, exuberant spirits. That those hard moments made a deep impression we can now see, for so many of them come to light in her stories, along with the happiness and the unexpected adventures which fall along the way of the seeker for her daily bread. One small episode reflects very significantly Louisa's own ideas about certain matters.

In *An Old-Fashioned Girl*, someone, in Polly's hearing, refers to her single festive frock, a black silk gown, as "that inevitable dress," and calls the girl "the little blackbird." Louisa herself put on record a similar incident. "People are remarking on how familiar my best black silk has become" she says in substance. "I shall either have to get another or go home to Concord. I am going home to Concord." Her reverence for social etiquette and conventional garb was not very great. Older people who can remember say that *An Old-Fashioned Girl* is an absolutely accurate picture of Boston society in her time, with all its small customs and habits and invariable laws of procedure. As we see Polly break through some of them and express her own opinions of others we understand fairly well what Louisa thought.

The story in its first form was very short, only seven chapters, but as before, a sequel was so loudly demanded that Louisa presently added the remainder, to make the present book. She found the characters amongst her legion of cousins and relatives in Boston and among her friends. No single person is directly recognizable but all have the mark of reality upon them.

She had worked so hard over the second part of *Little Women* as to be quite worn out, and to show, alas, that her strength had never come back to its old vigor. A little time before the war, her Cousin Lizzie Wells was ill and Louisa stayed with her to nurse her. Being free for a Sunday and having missed the train to Concord, she walked home, twenty miles, and went to a party in the evening. Such boundless energy as

216

that was never to come back to her. She was in fact never really well again after the hospital adventure. Although she was definitely ill through all the time that she was writing *An Old-Fashioned Girl*, she gave no hint of flagging spirits and made the story as gay as Louisa always was herself, when feeling her best.

The time had come when she had accomplished the greater part of what she had so long ago vowed that she would do. She had made her family safe and independent, she had given them comfort, and she had paid off all the old debts which ran back to the time of the Temple School. With the ordinary affairs of life attended to she turned to a larger and more pretentious dream which she had harbored long, as something impossibly remote. She would send May abroad to give her the artistic education which she felt that her sister's talents richly deserved. She knew just how May longed for travel, just as she herself had longed for it. Her own desire had been laboriously and inadequately fulfilled; May's wish should be answered in full measure, heaped and running over.

She consulted a friend, Miss Alice Bartlett, as to plans. Wise and generous Miss Bartlett had a glorious idea. She too was going abroad and she offered to take May as her guest if Louisa would go also. Such a thing as going herself had not crossed Louisa's mind. She pondered it — not long, for she was still Louisa — and decided to go.

All the delight which she had hoped to have on that first journey and had failed to find was hers now. Louisa was not well; she had worked so hard that she never was to have any full amount of bodily ease again. But she spent small time in lamentation over that. Beyond the ordinary gift of other people, she had the capacity for enjoying herself and for knowing when she was happy. She was not hurried past German castles now, or snatched away from picturesque French villages that she longed to explore, or carried on from beautiful, bright countrysides where she liked to linger and bask in the golden warmth of Italian spring. Laughter and light-heartedness attended the progress of these three congenial spirits wherever they went. She looked all about for Ladislas but she did not find him. Years later he was to come to America and she was to renew her knowledge of him but she did not see him now.

They landed at Brest and spent a sunny, delightful April in Brittany. As the summer came on they moved forward to Geneva. Europe was by this time in a turmoil on account of the Franco-Prussian War which broke out soon after they reached Switzerland. That glittering Emperor, Napoleon III, who had tried so hard to emulate the power and magnificence of his uncle, the great Buonaparte, was making his last, superhuman effort to win glory on the battlefield, and by so doing to instill new life into the dying legend of imperial glory. The Empress Eugenie was holding the reins of government at home, and amid the ominous muttering of a discontented populace, was keeping up the outward semblance of pomp and splendor. The Emperor was ill, suffering, beside himself with nervous excitement, but still dreaming of glory, while the crash of shells and cannon roared about him, the thundering German artillery which was to bring down the French empire forever.

"Poor old man," Louisa said of him, remembering how she had seen his Paris in its greatest glory. Switzerland was full of refugees; the Queen of Spain and her son were keeping Court in a hotel in Geneva, not far from Louisa. The three Americans were interested in the romance and excitement of such great changes but it all seemed very remote from them.

In the autumn they moved on to Italy. Louisa wrote home of lodging in a room with a marble floor, "green doors, red carpet, blue walls and yellow bed covers — all so gay. It was like sleeping in a rainbow." The whole journey seemed rainbow-colored in its untroubled happiness. It did not matter to Louisa that she had pain in her bones and was often worn out. The good company and the great sights about her were enough and more to counteract all that. She wrote home from Brittany. "Ye gods, how I do sleep here," a pathetic testimonial to how she had not slept for many months past. The beautiful journey helped her but it could not make her well. She told of how Miss Bartlett shopped briskly for antiques, May sketched with energy, and "I dawdled after them." It was a blessed relief to have time for dawdling.

While they were staying in Rome news reached them of the death of John Pratt, Anna's husband, leaving Louisa's sister with small means and with two little boys. Louisa was brokenhearted over her sister's grief but immediately took the steps which were characteristic of her. She took up the pen which she had meant to lay aside for a long vacation and resumed her writing, so that "John's death may not leave Anna and the dear little boys in want."

It was so that she undertook *Little Men*, and carried forward the account of the school at Plumfield, and the further chronicle, purely imaginary now, of the March family. She took no further joy in her holiday after that, since she felt that she was needed in Concord. It was decided that May should stay on for more study and that Louisa should go home.

Her father and Thomas Niles met her at the wharf, with news of the book. The manuscript of *Little Men*, arriving in the mail, almost unheralded from Rome, had been a tremendous surprise. The book was out the day Louisa got home, with such a prodigious number sold before publication that it had already achieved unprecedented honors for a story for young people. Her books had already begun to be translated into various languages. In our time, many have come to be read in practically every modern tongue.

It was always plain to Louisa, after she had been away, how feeble and old her mother seemed to become during her absence. It was true that Abba Alcott's iron strength was failing and that the change, unnoticed by those about her, was evident to any person who did not see her every day. Louisa vowed that she would never go far away from her again. She never did.

When May returned some months later, Louisa gave into her hands, with a sigh of relief, the task of keeping house in Concord. Fame threatened to become an occupation in itself and leave Louisa no time for actual living. The visitors and the letters and the autograph albums seemed to have no end. She was asked often to speak at schools and colleges and, having a definite interest in education, she agreed whenever she could. Some people were kind and she loved to meet them; some curious, and some merely intrusive. Many who came seemed to have no idea that Miss Alcott might like a little privacy nor did it seem to occur to them that she must have some quiet if she were to produce any more books. To the infinitely repeated question:

"Dear Miss Alcott, are you writing anything now?" she was tempted often to answer bitterly: "How can I?"

The years slipped by pleasantly, however, quite a number of them, without great event. *Little Men* was nearly as great a success as *Little Women*. Under demand for more books, Louisa again brought out her novel, *Success*, renamed *Work*, and got it ready for publication. Two years later she wrote *Eight Cousins* and one year after that its sequel, *Rose in Bloom*. *Work* was widely discussed as *Mood* had been, but with no long-lived enthusiasm. The two young people's books, however, were universally beloved. Into *Eight Cousins* and its sequel she has put the general atmosphere of the enormous May connection, everyone interested in everyone else, the elders observing with watchful care just how the younger ones were growing up in "these dreadful modern times." Part of the magic of Louisa's charm for young people surely lies in the fact that she sees things through their eyes, that she depicts the ups and downs of the early adventures of life, all from the young point of view. The youthful readers all feel, entirely, that Louisa is *on their side*.

Much more of the time now she remained in Concord, so that she might be near her mother. Occasionally as she walked along the shady streets she would meet that old comrade, Cy, with whom she had played when she was small, who got her to jump off the beam of the barn. They never could greet each other without suddenly bursting into laughter, for the memories of those hazardous days were still common property between the brown-faced farmer, veteran of the war, and tall, stately Miss Alcott, famous authoress. Occasionally, when she felt herself able, she would go to Boston for a little, and she once spent several months in New York. In Boston she still occasionally acted in private theatricals with all of her old spirit. There was a great fair to raise money for the preservation of the Old South Church. Louisa was the life of the whole undertaking, her special show, "Mrs. Jarley's Waxworks," with herself as Mrs. Jarley, being a marvelous performance which was repeated every day for a week. She was tired out by it and at the end so hoarse that she could barely speak; but in spite of everything she threw tremendous zest into every scene and was an uproarious success.

When she could she went to talk to schools although she never could accept a quarter of the invitations which poured in upon her. She went to Philadelphia and spoke at the Germantown Academy, the surviving school which, as has been said, was born out of the plan of Reuben Haines. The boys all cheered her as she passed up School House Lane. She saw Wyck again, where she had played when she was so very little; she was taken to see her birthplace, a very old house now and soon to be demolished. At the house of her hostess, she was waited on by a delegation of young persons, grandchildren of those small pupils whom her father had taught. The group of little girls overwhelmed her with questions as to whether Beth really had scarlet fever, why Laurie did not marry Jo, who was Mr. Lawrence. She answered every query, wrote in all the autograph albums, and kissed such of those who insisted upon it. So tired was she when this interview was over that she could hardly manage to answer a second summons which came up to her room a little later. This time she was asked to come down to speak to a delegation of little boys. Unwilling to refuse any request, she came down and found only two young gentlemen, both very shy, and both sitting on the edges of their chairs. Conversation did not go forward very easily but they were at last persuaded to tell what they had come to ask.

"Please, were the pillow fights real?"

"They were," Louisa assured them. "They were always on Saturday nights, just before the clean cases were put on for Sunday."

That was all they wished to know and they took their departure, completely satisfied.

Louisa had sent May to Europe once more, during these quiet years, but was overwhelmingly glad to get her back again and to avail herself of the efficient help which May always managed to be. Abba Alcott was really an old woman now, so feeble as to need much care and to call forth great anxiety amongst those who loved her. She was happy and serene but she was evidently not to be with them a great deal longer. In September 1876, Louisa arranged for the third time that May should go abroad. She needed a holiday, Louisa said. It was such a happiness to May to have that artist's life which she craved; it was such a joy to Louisa to give it to her. This time, there was no question of Louisa's going also. The two daughters could not possibly be away at the same time.

May sailed on a windy September day, some such day as that on which Louisa had first set out on her own travels. The two sisters went to the wharf together. Separations were difficult in this devoted family and were never gone through without pain and misgiving, no matter what golden promise lay in the plans which brought the parting. There was a little prayer which Louisa said to herself many times through her whole life,

"God help us all and keep us for one another."

She had said it on that day when she set out in the coach from Walpole to try her fortune in Boston. She had said it on the day of her going away to Washington to offer all her strength and eagerness to the service of her country. She said it now as the ship drew out from the dock and gathered way. May, with her blue cape blowing out in the breeze, stood at the rail to wave good-bye. Louisa waved in return, gayly and bravely, her tall figure bending a little to the wind, the tendrils of her chestnut hair lifting, her face bright with the splendid hopes which sped this beloved sister on her way.

It is so, I think, that we should always remember her. At that moment life gave her, perhaps, the supreme amount of what she had asked of it. She had won security for all those whom she loved so much, peace and happiness for her family, this final gift which she was able to make to May. That was all that Louisa had wished for; but she had something more. Warm in her heart was the knowledge that thousands of people loved her, people whom she had never seen, whose names she was never to hear.

Fame during a lifetime is something to win; but fame and affection which are to last a hundred years are seldom earned. These Louisa had, with a richness of deserving about which we love to think, as we look back at her gay-spirited, vivid, and hopeful, waving, not to May, but to us, across the century.

# CHAPTER TEN

# Happy Ending

WHENEVER BRONSON ALCOTT USED TO SET off for his lecturing journeys to the West there was always a good deal of flurry in the old Orchard House. May would tie his neckcloth and give him a final brushing, Abba Alcott would offer him last reminders of the ways in which he was to take care of himself, Louisa would go through his bag to make sure that she had packed everything. New shirts, socks in great quantities, warm flannels, the sage himself in a new overcoat! Even after years of prosperity Louisa always found it astonishing that they should at last have everything that they really needed. There was a family saying, "poor as poverty, but serene as heaven," which well described their state in the earlier days. No matter what they lacked they always made merry over it. Now there was just the same hilarity and gay-hearted affection, while behind it all was the new, solid sense of well-being, so that even though old age was upon the elders of that house, there would never again be want and anxiety.

It was Louisa alone who did the most of the preparation for departure now, since May was away and their mother grown so feeble. The lectures were more and more of a success every year. Bronson said that it was due to his daughter's fame that he was so cordially received and declared that he was "riding in Louisa's chariot." That was not entirely true. His later achievements well bore out the first spirited statement made on that cold night in the shabby Boston house so many years ago, the unquenched assertion that though he had earned only one dollar on the first expedition, he had opened the way and would do better another time. It was with pride and confidence that they saw him go, Louisa doing the active work of getting him ready, her mother watching in quiet pleasure.

Abba Alcott was slowly slipping into the rest and peace which were to be greater even than any Louisa could give. She was cheerful and free from suffering through weeks and months of failing. Bronson had come home and Louisa's arms were close about her when she finally went away. How strange it was to be in that household and know that the strong spirit which had ruled it so long was absent.

It was hard that May was not there to help

them bear the loss and the loneliness which came after, a sense of desolation which Louisa found it so difficult to accept. Her greatest tribute to her mother is perhaps in her statement of what was and what was not taken from life in *Little Women*. "Mrs. March is all true, only not half good enough." When Bronson set off on his next journey, May was not there, Abba was not there, but Louisa and Anna had joined forces to face their sorrow.

They did not stay on in the Orchard House after Abba Alcott's final illness came upon her. Louisa had never really liked the place, could never overcome the disappointment that Elizabeth had not lived to enjoy it, could never forget her own hideous struggle with illness in that upper room. For some time she had wanted to buy a house for Anna and the two boys, one nearer to the town. She finally purchased the house on Main Street which had belonged to Henry Thoreau and thither they had moved before her mother left them. It is a smaller, more compact, more comfortable dwelling, neat and square and white, like its dignified Concord neighbors. The Pratt family, Anna's children and grandchildren, lived there after them; so that the last of the Alcott kindred occupy it still.

The final book of Louisa's which her mother read was one of a most unusual kind. Louisa never could quite put aside her taste for startling events and her love for writing tales which bordered on the fantastic. The firm of Roberts Brothers was getting out a succession of novels which they called the "No Name Series." The books were all by well-known authors of the day but were published without names, so that the public should have the excitement of a little mystery and some exercise at guessing who had written them. Louisa was delighted to be asked to contribute a book and plunged into the composition of *A Modern Mephistopheles.*

She had always loved Goethe and his powerful version of the story of Faust. In this tale she gives her conception of a parallel with the Faust legend, enacted in her own time. She enjoyed it enormously and was delighted over the mystification which followed its appearance. People would not easily guess that the author of *Little Women* could have produced this emotional and tragic novel and were greatly puzzled. In time of course the secret was revealed and the book was finally published with her own name. Her mother got as much enjoyment out of the small stir of excitement as did Louisa. When the novel was finished, Louisa began another story for boys and girls, *Under the Lilacs.* Abba Alcott did not live to read it.

May did not come home on the occasion of

her mother's death; instead she sent great and happy news of her own. She was to be married to Ernest Nieriker, a Swiss, whom she had met in London. It seemed an exceedingly happy combination of congenial spirits, so that May's joyous letters were a source of great comfort to Louisa in the year that followed, a sad, hard, lonely year; since Louisa must work to care for them all at home and her own health was growing more and more precarious. She longed to go to visit May as her sister urged, but was not well enough for any such journey to be possible.

Just before leaving the Orchard House, they had all been delighted over an honor which had come to Bronson Alcott. The School of Philosophy, long talked of, was finally established, the meetings held in a wooden building put up in the grounds of the old house. Here summer sessions were held and all the sages of Concord, Alcott, Emerson, and other members of a very goodly company gave forth their wisdom. It was well attended, people coming from all directions, knowing that this was a rare opportunity. The great feature of the summer was Emerson Day, when real tribute was paid to that man who had influenced so many, had done so much good, and had been such an unfaltering friend to those who so greatly needed him. One more act of friendship he was to be called upon to perform for his dear Alcotts. It was the hardest of all.

A year after May's marriage, tidings arrived of a further event. Louisa had waited long for her namesake but she now need wait no more. Here was young Louisa again, Louisa May Nieriker. May was so happy, she seemed to have nothing left for which to ask, except to see her sister. "Such a tugging at my heart to see May," Louisa says, as an echo to that wish, and spoke more than once of a heaviness of misgivings about her beloved sister.

It was about a month later that Louisa was called downstairs in the new house to see Mr. Emerson. One glance at his white, infinitely distressed face, warned her of why he had come. Ernest Nieriker had sent him a cablegram whose contents he was to give to Louisa. The fateful paper was in his hand.

"My child, I wish I could prepare you, but — alas — alas — " His voice broke and he could do no more than give her the telegram.

"I *am* prepared," Louisa answered steadily. All her old resolute spirit came to her aid, as she read the news which was to hurt her almost beyond bearing. May was dead, gay, carefree May, whose happiness had so brightened life for all of them. It was scarcely to be believed.

Thus, when life seemed completely settled for

Louisa, with nothing before her but the steady progress of the years, there came a complete change. Her mother had given her the task of caring for her father; she had expected that and was fulfilling the undertaking with her whole heart. Now May also had told those about her that, if she did not live, her sister was to have her baby. And so young Louisa Nieriker came to be Louisa's own, and henceforth the household was to revolve around her.

Louisa could not go to Switzerland to get May's little daughter, as she longed to do, but sent a trusted woman to bring her home. Sophie Nieriker came also, May's sister-in-law. When they arrived some months later Louisa was waiting at the wharf where she had stood to watch May sail away. The captain came off the ship, carrying a yellow-haired baby, a little portrait of May, come to comfort Louisa. She was royally welcomed and carried home and many times at night Louisa would go into her room to look at her in her small bed, to make sure that she was really there. Louisa still could scarcely credit the idea that May was gone and that Lulu was there in her place.

One of the ways in which children are a comfort is their ability to keep everyone occupied and absorbed in them. Lulu was no easy child to manage; she was Louisa over again in her stormy moods and her inflexible will. Louisa had hoped to take all the care of her; but that was impossible, owing to her own lack of health. She kept house for Lulu, bought a summer cottage by the sea for Lulu, and later a house in Louisburg Square; she made little songs and sang them to Lulu and wrote brief stories for her.

It was during the second year after Lulu arrived that Concord suffered the loss of two commanding spirits whose presence had made history there. Ralph Waldo Emerson died in April, 1882, a man so deeply mourned that it hardly seemed possible that Concord could continue to be Concord without him. Great things he did, and small, and all of them good. Not only was he a leader of the thought of his time, wise and temperate in judgment, when others were running headlong into new ideas. He was also the help and standby of many a struggling genius, many another besides the Alcotts. "He has a sweet way of bestowing gifts, on the table under a book or behind a candlestick, when he thinks Father wants a little money and no one will help him earn," Louisa said of him. The time for such need had passed for the Alcotts but the memory of his kindness would never grow dim. It was on his account that the Alcotts lived in Concord; it was he who oversaw Louisa's reading and taught her much of what she knew about life and people. Always, he was a sure counselor in any time of distress; he understood and appreciated every member of the gifted family and was a help to each one in turn. One day, as he and Louisa were speaking of Bronson, he exclaimed:

"Louisa, your father might have talked with Plato!" It was the tribute to her beloved father which, above all others, Louisa appreciated the most and remembered longest.

After Emerson was gone, the real Bronson Alcott did not abide long without him. In the autumn of that same year he suffered a stroke of paralysis and although he lived on, he was feeble, almost helpless, and never really himself again. He was happy and, with his quiet spirit, apparently at peace within himself, but his active life was over.

Louisa and Anna took devoted care of him. They did not spend much time in Concord after Mr. Emerson died. Louisa liked Boston and still, in spite of the discomforts of her health, was able to go about, see friends, and take part in the affairs which interested her. She was always an ardent supporter of women's rights, even though at that time votes for women seemed impossibly far away. Her old interest in acting never diminished so that she went to the theater whenever she could. She recorded seeing the great actress Ellen Terry. She did not put into her journal how she and Miss Terry were guests of honor at a luncheon soon afterward, and how the actress, being asked for an autograph, wrote down, "My ambition is gratified; I sit at the same table and behold with my own eyes, the authoress of *Little Women*."

Through all of this time Louisa still wrote steadily. The book upon which she was working while her mother was ill, *Under the Lilacs*, was published the year after *A Modern Mephistopheles*. Although she planned various novels later — indeed, her mind was always a seething ferment of plans — she never wrote another book for grown-up readers. It was hard to go on writing *Under the Lilacs* while her heart was so bowed down with sorrow, but she finished it and made of it her usual cheerful, lively tale.

It was at the time of May's death that she struggled to the end of *Jack and Jill*, another story apparently quite unclouded by the grief which its author was facing. This book has to do with Concord and Concord children but reflects, it seems, the little invalid girl whom Louisa taught in those first years of breadwinning. It appeared the year that Lulu came from Switzerland. From that time forth most of Louisa's published work was short stories brought out in various collections. Through the whole of those final years, however, she was working on *Jo's Boys*.

That book seems to be the background of

everything that she did, to be connected with all of the events which followed. She tried to work on it in the cottage at Nonquit, whither Anna and her boys and Lulu and her nurse, and Bronson Alcott all used to come for the summer. It was a flimsy little wooden house, with a tower and all the fantastic architecture which that period could put into hastily built wooden dwellings. It had one glorious feature in Louisa's eyes: "It was without the curse of a kitchen." How many hot hours she had toiled over cookstove and dishpans to keep her family properly provided for! Now she need do it no more, and she did not even want the faintest reminder of such necessity. She made games and dramas for the children to act — the little girls who came to play with Lulu. But she did not make progress with *Jo's Boys*.

In the pleasant, sunny house in Louisburg Square, which she took so that they might all be together in Boston, she congratulated herself that Lulu was so pleased with her nursery and her father with his pleasant room. There is no mention of a study or of any privacy for herself, where she could write in peace. So even here, even in spite of the troubled urging of Thomas Niles, *Jo's Boys* did not go forward. She was obliged to leave the others at last and take a room at the Bellevue, with John Pratt for more quiet company. Anna's two boys were grown now and working in the firm of Roberts Brothers. Later she adopted John, the younger, and gave him the name of Alcott. It was necessary that she should have someone to be her direct legal heir to inherit her copyrights when she was gone. John was very close to her and was with her more than were the others.

She began going in the summer to the Mountain House near Princeton, Massachusetts. Across the road from the hotel was a cottage where she could have quiet and be free from the eternal staring of the people who liked to hunt down celebrities. Her health was more and more broken, but she was still erect, commanding, and overflowing with friendship and good spirits. She was still, as always, interested in girls who were making their own way, and she liked to gather the working girls of the hotel staff, bring them all to her room, and hear them discuss their problems and ambitions. At different times she wrote many short stories on the subject of girls who face the difficulty of breadwinning, the most of them being gathered in the collection, *A Garland for Girls.* In the tale, out of the number, called "Poppies and Wheat," we see something of her experiences as a traveling companion on that first expedition to Europe. There were at the hotel mentioned two little girls from the West, very devoted and very busy with their dolls. She put them into *Jo's Boys*; she was finally bringing it to an end.

The story is a sequel to *Little Men* and has to do with Plumfield and the further fortunes of the boys gathered there and of the March family. For the interruptions and the long intervals between the terms of writing, she apologized, in the preface, saying that the book cannot be as good a piece of work as she desired. Louisa's prefaces were always modest; they always showed her as seeing the faults of the book rather than taking satisfaction in its true worth. In the last lines she said with finality, "The curtain falls forever on the March family."

The Mountain House was built upon the slope of an old friend, Wachusett. From her window Louisa could look down upon a valley which had lived in her memory through all the changing years; she could see the Still River, the broad sloping meadows, rising to rugged hillsides; she could see Fruitlands. What must she have thought as she sat looking upon that scene of bitter struggle, where her father's and her mother's hearts came so near to being broken, where she herself had first awakened to the sense of responsibility? The whole valley was pink with June laurel now, so peaceful and so still, as though no desperate battles of the spirit could ever have taken place amid that serene landscape.

She was so glad to be coming to the end of her book. She put down her pen and sat looking from the window for a long time. She knew that, once this was finished, she was to write no more.

Louisa was never to see old age. She died, after steadily increasing illness, two years later, on the sixth of March, 1888. The last summer she spent on Wachusett again, not writing, but sitting quietly at the window — looking down on Fruitlands. Later, a few days before her own end, she stood by the bedside of her father, who was fading imperceptibly into death as a long life does, when nearing its final limit. She was too ill to stay with him and, while driving home, she caught cold with fatal effect. When she died, she did not know that Bronson Alcott had gone just before her. What she did know was that she had taken care of him to the very last of his needing her, that she had been able to guard and protect and watch over the entire family. That, indeed, was happy ending; that was the whole of what she had wanted from life — just to take care of them all.

# CHRONOLOGY OF
# LOUISA MAY ALCOTT'S
# LIFE

BECAUSE THE STORY OF LOUISA ALCOTT'S LIFE DOES NOT seem to call for the continual mention of dates, yet because such definite matters are necessary for reference, this table is given. It shows the time of the principal events in this account.

1799   Bronson Alcott was born, November twenty-ninth, in Wolcott, Connecticut.

1800   Abigail (Abba) May Alcott was born, October eighth, in Boston.

1830   Bronson Alcott and Abba May were married, May twenty-third, in King's Chapel, Boston.
       December. Bronson and Abba Alcott came to Germantown.

1831   Germantown, Pine Place. Anna Alcott was born, March sixteenth.
       Reuben Haines died, October.

1832   Germantown, Pine Place. Louisa was born, November twenty-ninth.

1833   Germantown, Pine Place. The Alcotts moved to Philadelphia, March.

1834   The Alcotts moved to Boston. The Temple School opened in September.

1835   Boston, Number 26 Front Street. Elizabeth Sewall Alcott was born.

1836   Boston, Front Street.

1837   Boston, Cottage Place. "Conversations on the Gospel," by Bronson Alcott, was published.

1839  Boston, Beach Street. The Temple School was closed.

1840  Concord, Hosmer Cottage. Abba May Alcott was born.

1841  Concord, Hosmer Cottage.

1842  Concord, Hosmer Cottage. Bronson Alcott sailed for England in May. He returned in October.

1843  Fruitlands, June to December.

1844  Still River, Massachusetts. In the spring the Alcotts returned to Concord, staying with the Hosmers.

1845  Concord, Hillside. In the winter of 1845–1846, Anna and Louisa went to John Hosmer's school. Louisa began to write plays.

1846  Concord, Hillside.

1847  Concord, Hillside.

1848  Concord, Hillside. Louisa opened her school in the barn. She wrote the stories, published later as *Flower Fables*, for Ellen Emerson. The Alcotts moved to Boston.

1849  Boston. In the summer, Atkinson Street. In the winter, Dedham Street.

1850  Boston, Dedham Street.

1851  Boston, High Street. Louisa "went out to service."

1852  Boston, High Street. Louisa's first story was printed.

1853  Boston, Pinckney Street. Louisa and Anna had a school in the parlor.

1854  Boston, Pinckney Street.

1855  Louisa went for the summer to Walpole, New Hampshire. The whole family moved there in the autumn. *Flower Fables* appeared as a book. Louisa went to Boston alone.

1856  Walpole. June, Elizabeth and May were ill with scarlet fever. Louisa spent the summer in Walpole, returned to Boston in November.

1857  Louisa was in Boston, at Mrs. Reed's, Pinckney Street. October, the family moved to Concord to the house near the Town Hall. They bought Orchard House.

1858    Concord. March, Elizabeth died. The family lived
        temporarily at Hillside. Anna became engaged to
        John Bridge Pratt. They moved to Orchard House in
        July. Louisa returned to Boston in October.

1859    Boston. Sewing, writing, and teaching.

1860    Boston. Anna was married, May twenty-third.

1860    Boston. Louisa began *Moods* in August in Concord.
        Theodore Parker died.

1861    Boston. Wrote, in the summer in Concord, on *Moods*
        and *Success*. War was declared between the North
        and the South.

1862    Boston. Taught in a kindergarten school. November,
        Louisa volunteered as a nurse, and December, went
        to Georgetown Hospital.

1863    Washington. January, Louisa was taken home ill.
        March, Anna's son was born, Frederic Alcott Pratt.
        "Hospital Sketches" were published in the *Common-
        wealth*. In August they were printed as a book by
        Redpath.

1864    Concord. Louisa wrote on *Moods* and *Success*. *Moods*
        was published.

1865    Concord. Louisa sailed for Europe, July nineteenth.
        She met Ladislas Wisniewski in Vevey, November.
        Anna's second son, John Sewall Pratt, was born.

1866    Nice, Paris, London. Louisa returned to Concord in
        July.

1867    Boston, Number 6 Hayward Place. Thomas Niles
        asked Louisa for a "book for girls."

1868    Boston, Hayward Place and Brookline Street. Thomas
        Niles asked again for "a book for girls." Louisa
        began *Little Women* in May in Concord, finished the
        first twelve chapters in June, finished the whole in
        July. *Little Women* was published in October,
        Louisa began the sequel November first.

1869    Boston, Chauncey Street. The second volume of
        *Little Women* was sent to Roberts Brothers on New
        Year's Day and published in May.

1870    Boston. Louisa began *An Old-Fashioned Girl*, which was published in March. Louisa sailed April second for Brest.

1871    Italy and Rome. John Pratt died. Louisa wrote *Little Men*. Louisa came home in June. *Little Men* was published in June.

1872    Boston, Allston Street. *Shawl-straps* was published.

1873    Boston, Allston Street. Louisa finished *Success*, renamed *Work*. *Work* was published.

1874    Boston, "At the South End, near the Park." Anna, Mrs. Alcott, and Anna's boys were with Louisa. December, Louisa finished *Eight Cousins*.

1875    Boston, Bellevue Hotel. *Eight Cousins* was published. November and December, at the Bath Hotel, New York.

1876    Boston. Louisa wrote *Rose in Bloom* in Concord in the summer. *Rose in Bloom* was published in November. The Thoreau House was bought for Anna and the boys. May sailed for Europe, September ninth.

1877    Boston, Bellevue Hotel. Louisa wrote *A Modern Mephistopheles*, which was published in April. Louisa began *Under the Lilacs*. November twenty-fifth, Mrs. Alcott died, in Concord.

1878    Concord. March twenty-second, May was married in London to Ernest Nieriker.

1879    Boston, Bellevue Hotel. Louisa began *Jack and Jill*. November eighth, Louisa May Nieriker was born. December twenty-ninth, May died.

1880    Boston, Bellevue Hotel. *Jack and Jill* was published. Summer, the School of Philosophy was opened in Concord. September, Lulu Nieriker arrived in Boston.

1881    Boston and Concord. Louisa wrote only short stories and was absorbed in Lulu.

1882    Boston, Bellevue Hotel, and Concord. April twenty-seventh, Emerson died. Louisa began *Jo's Boys*. In

246

the autumn, Bronson Alcott was stricken with paralysis.

1883    Boston, Concord, and Nonquit. *Jo's Boys.*

1884    Boston, Concord, and Nonquit. Louisa bought the cottage at Nonquit.

1885    Boston, Louisburg Square; Concord; Princeton, Massachusetts. *Jo's Boys.*

1886    Boston; Concord; and Princeton, Massachusetts. Louisa finished *Jo's Boys.* The book was published.

1887    Boston.

1888    Boston. *A Garland for Girls* was published. Bronson Alcott died, March fourth. Louisa died, March sixth.